**Amos L. Howard, Sr.**

# Legacy Matters

**Legacy Matters**

All Scripture quotations, unless otherwise indicated, are taken from the Holy Bible New International Version®, NIV® Copyright 1973, 1978, 1984 by International Bible Society; the King James Version; the Amplified Version; and The Message Bible. Used by permission.

Printed in the United States of America
Amos L. Howard Ministries
102 Ridley Street
Smyrna, TN 37167



ISBN: 978-1-7365882-3-9

# TABLE OF CONTENTS

# TRIBUTES

Carolyn E. Peebles was a woman whose life exemplified strength, faith, and purpose, leaving a legacy that will echo for generations. Born into humble beginnings in Murfreesboro, Tennessee, she grew to become a pioneer, often breaking barriers as both the first woman and first Black woman in roles traditionally closed to her. Carolyn's career spanned from Nissan to Living Truth Christian Center, where she served with excellence and commitment. She owned and operated About My Father's Business and FOYA Travel, driven by a vision to empower others with her gifts in finance, administration, and event planning. Beyond her work, Carolyn was deeply devoted to her community, holding numerous positions on boards and community initiatives, always with the heart of a servant. Apostle Amos, Dr. Yolanda, and the Howard family loved Carolyn deeply and cherish her memory, thanking God for her faithful service of love poured out for the church and community. Her faith and love were the cornerstones of her life, touching everyone she met. Carolyn's legacy is not just in her achievements but in the countless lives she uplifted, the doors she opened, and the faith she embodied. She showed us that legacy truly matters—not only in what we accomplish but in the live we inspire and the love we leave behind.

**Mark E. Turner: A Legacy of Wisdom, Friendship, and Faith**

Some people come into your life and leave an imprint so deep that their impact lasts for generations. Mark E. Turner was one of those people for me. I met Mark at an auction, and from that moment, my life changed forever. What started as a chance encounter turned into a divine connection—Mark became more than a mentor; he was a friend, a brother, and a father figure in the real estate world. His knowledge was unmatched, his wisdom invaluable, and his generosity beyond measure. At one time, he was the youngest real estate broker in the State of Tennessee, but his influence extended far beyond titles and accolades. Mark was a family man through and through, a man of integrity, and a businessman who led with both strategy and heart.

Mark not only taught me the ropes of real estate, but he was directly responsible for some of my most valuable acquisitions. He was my unofficial maintenance man—always willing, always present, always offering his expertise. I honestly don't know what I would have done in my early real estate days without his guidance. He was one of my angels, a God-send who helped shape the trajectory of my success. Mark didn't just grow tomatoes in his garden; he cultivated wisdom, opportunity, and lasting relationships. His love for his wife, Kim Turner, was evident, and I am equally grateful for her impact on my life and family.

Mark's life reminds me of Proverbs 27:17, *"As iron sharpens iron, so one person sharpens another."* He sharpened me, challenged me, and uplifted me. I love and miss him tremendously, but his legacy will never fade. Because of Mark and Kim Turner, my family's legacy is forever changed. His imprint on my life is eternal, and I thank God for the gift of his friendship and mentorship.

# FORWARD

Proverbs 13:22 NKJV says, ***"A good man leaves an inheritance to his children's children, But the wealth of the sinner is stored up for the righteous."*** As He taught Abraham, Isaac, and Jacob, God expects His children to create and accumulate wealth that will bless future generations. Our family legacies, as believers, should be rich in faith *and* material assets. But, because too few Christians have been taught about legacy, generational wealth, and God's covenant of increase, too many believers have not fully received and enjoyed all that Jesus died to provide them. Thankfully, Apostle Amos L. Howard — a gifted ministry leader and teacher — has answered the call to teach this topic within the Body of Christ.

Using simple language and real-life examples that will appeal to readers of all ages and stages of life, *Legacy Matters: Ensuring Your Legacy Through Intentional Living* is a thoughtful and detailed work that reveals the importance of legacy to God and every child of God who wants to glorify their heavenly Father.

Apostle Howard shares without apology or blame how he grew up in an environment that "normalized" poverty and lack. As a child, "*Poverty felt normal*," he writes. "*That is why today, I have such an appreciation for what God has blessed me to be able to do for my children and grandchildren and the opportunities He has afforded me to provide a better life for my family.*"

*Legacy Matters* is an inspired and timely resource with over one hundred and thirty actionable wisdom keys for this generation to create a lasting legacy. Defining legacy as "***the footprint of your spirit left in the universe,***" Apostle Howard inspires the reader to live a life of bold abundance with intention and impact.

As he writes, ***"Success is NOT an accident. Nothing just happens!... Life is meant to be lived on purpose and in purpose. The question is, how do you want to be remembered when you leave this life?"***

We will all have to answer this question one day, and I believe this book can help you find the answer.

*Dr. Bill Winston, Founder and Pastor*
*Living Word Christian Center*
*Forest Park, Illinois*

# PREFACE

*Legacy Matters* is a blueprint and guide to help put your legal and personal affairs in order to help navigate the process of telling your life story. It teaches you how to go within and examine your life, identifying your strengths, weaknesses, accomplishments, failures, ups and downs. This process forms a powerful legacy to leave for your spouse, children, grandchildren, great grandchildren, family, community and the world.

You are in control of the narrative of your life. You have the power and authority to tell the world who you are and leave a legacy that speaks to the essence of your being. *Legacy Matters* empowers you to tell your story how you want it to be told.

*Legacy Matters* is for those who may not be aware of the power of legacy, those who may not understand the dynamics of legacy, and those who have not thought about legacy from a perspective of power. This book speaks to the young adult just starting to understand who they are, all the way up to the 100 year-old who is just coming into the awareness that their life matters. This book is for those who have plenty and those who think they have very little. This book is for me. This book is for you. **YOUR LEGACY MATTERS!**

Every day of your life contributes to the legacy you leave behind. Therefore, you must be deliberate in creating the story of your life that speaks to the truth of who you are, and the contribution God created you to be in the earth. This means being intentional about the story you want to be told about you, not only while you are alive but also after you leave this life. Your life could continue to resonate even into eternity. Those who meet you in heaven should be able to look back and see the full, meaningful life you led and the lasting effects of the truth that God deposited in you.

My divine calling is to assist people in deliberately planning, processing, and preparing for what God purposed for them to do in this life, and what they are to leave in the earth when they depart this life. It is about ensuring that whatever you desire to achieve or leave behind is done intentionally, encouraging you to give serious consideration to legacy and what it truly means to live a full, meaningful life. Living a full life entails thoughtful contemplation about legacy and how you want to be remembered both in life and in death. I am committed to helping others embrace the wisdom that life can be lived purposefully and meaningfully. We are called to be responsible stewards of the life God has granted us, ensuring that we finish our course and finish strong.

**Allow me to share a little bit of my story...**

*Much of my childhood is a blur to me. However, I remember growing up poor. I remember this not because we lived in poor conditions but because of my understanding of poverty today and what I have accomplished in my life. As a child, I was part of the welfare system. We relied on government assistance to provide our basic needs. We received vouchers for clothing. I remember going to the store to buy candy or some other small item just so that we could get the change to purchase the things that we could not purchase with food stamps.*

*I was raised in a two-parent household, which had its own unique challenges. I recall the social worker's periodic visits to our home. There could be no sign of a man living there, so my father would have to make sure that all of his clothes were out the house. I remember feeling inferior because my parents could not afford name-brand clothes like the other children wore. My uncle, who is only a year older than me, lived a very different life. He had opportunities available to him that I never had. Despite all of that, my parents did an incredible job of camouflaging just how poor we really were.*

*I remember our home being destroyed by fire and having to wear hand-me-downs that were given to us by members of our community. Dining out was a rare occurrence, as we never really had the opportunity to explore different kinds of foods. That was not an option. Roast beef was a staple in our household. I remember eating government cheese, and cereal with powdered milk and water. I spent my childhood in the projects in Dodge City, a neighborhood known for its challenges back then and still considered troubled today. My father, a pastor and preacher, often moved us to different states, which added another layer of complexity to my upbringing. That was my world.*

*What amazes me is that as a child I was anesthetized to the extent of our poverty. Poverty felt normal. That is why today, I have such an appreciation for what God has blessed me to be able to do for my children and grandchildren and the opportunities He has afforded me to provide a better life for my family. To this day, I still find myself working to overcome that ingrained spirit of poverty.*

*I remember my mother buying Christmas gifts that she could not afford. Christmas was a big time in our home, and my mother was beyond generous. My mother has twelve siblings. She would buy gifts not only for all her brothers and sisters but also for their children, and if they had children, she would buy gifts for them too. My mother would wrap all the gifts in the funny pages from the newspaper because she said fancy wrapping paper was unnecessary since we would just tear the gifts open anyway. Despite our financial challenges, my mother was determined to celebrate Christmas every year.*

*As I moved into adulthood, I realized that poverty is a spirit, and it is one of the hardest spirits to break. Poor is a mindset. The spirit of poverty is evident when people become so accustomed to their past conditions that they struggle to adapt to their improved circumstances. For years, successful writer and filmmaker, Tyler Perry, lived well below his means, despite his current success,. He grew up poor. In an interview, he explained that it had not occurred to him to live differently because he was still influenced by his upbringing.*

*Poverty is a learned behavior, a mindset that originates from experiences of not having enough. This mentality can dominate your thoughts even when your financial situation has vastly improved. Living with a scarcity mindset for a long time can make it difficult to shake off the fear of returning to a state of insufficiency, regardless of your current status.*

*One day, I had a conversation with a young businesswoman from Sudan. She owns a boutique and hair braiding business in Tennessee. Her hair braiding business afforded her the opportunity to put her two sisters through school. She is remarkably successful, having sustained her business for ten years. Despite her achievements and being notably successful within her community, our discussion about the potential for even greater financial success revealed a different challenge. When the idea of having a surplus of $50,000 was mentioned, she was overwhelmed to the point of tears. This highlights a different kind of poverty, a mental barrier to envisioning and accepting greater financial success, even for those who have already achieved much. We experienced a breakthrough during our conversation. She began to understand how she had been limiting herself. There seems to be a systemic issue where societal labels of poverty align with a spiritual system that perpetuates poverty. This system affects us emotionally, mentally, and often spiritually by creating a scarcity mindset that influences many aspects of our lives.*

*To combat my own scarcity mindset, I adopted a practice of indulgence when dining out. If I see multiple dishes on the menu that interest me, I may order two or three entrees just for the experience of tasting them, whether it is a five-star restaurant or a no-star restaurant. The servers in the restaurants often comment on the quantity of food I order, but my family understands why I do it. I do this not only to enjoy the food but to challenge the poverty mentality that once constrained me. Psalm 34:8 says, "O taste and see that the Lord is good." I now embrace the opportunity to savor life's offerings, reinforcing a mindset of abundance over scarcity.*

Listen... success is NOT an accident. Nothing just happens! Life is intentional. Living is intentional. Leaving a powerful and impactful legacy is intentional. Life is meant to be lived "on purpose and in purpose." The question is, how do you want to be remembered when you leave this life?

From the moment we open our eyes to a brand new day, we are presented with countless opportunities to live life - but are you living life "on purpose" or are you merely existing? The possibility of living our lives "on purpose" and "in purpose" is not just a catchy phrase. It is a riveting idea that can redefine our lives and our perceptions of happiness and success. Life lived "on purpose" means being conscious of our actions, choices, and decisions. It means taking deliberate steps towards your goals, dreams, and passions rather than letting life just happen to you. It is when we wake up each day with enthusiasm and determination, fully aware that every moment, every choice, and every action has significance and potential to create a ripple effect in our lives and the world around us.

On the other hand, life lived "in purpose" is to find and embrace our unique calling and passion in life. It is about recognizing our strengths, talents, and passions, and aligning them with our actions and goals. To live life "in purpose" means to utilize our gifts to contribute to the world in a meaningful way, whether it is as grand as starting an organization, or as simple as spreading kindness and positivity.

Living life "on purpose" and "in purpose" is not a one-time decision. It is a commitment that requires time, patience, and growth. It is a journey that requires conscious effort to make sense of your experiences, learn from your failures and successes, and continually discover and embrace who you are and who you aspire to be. So, how do you start living life on purpose and in purpose? Start by asking yourself these three questions…

***1. What am I passionate about?***
***2. What are my strengths?***
***3. How can I make a difference?***

Reflect on these answers, mold your life around them and watch how life unfolds beautifully. Remember, the ultimate fulfillment we seek is not found somewhere else, in someone else, or at some other time - it is born from the realization that the life we want is the life we choose to live on purpose and in purpose. Wake up each day with a zeal to make a difference, to learn, and to grow. That is the truest and most fulfilling way to live, because you and your legacy matters.

***Prayer And Confession for Your Legacy!***

***Heavenly Father,***

***I come before You with a heart open to Your wisdom, guidance, and divine purpose for my life. Thank You for entrusting me with the gift of influence,wealth, and the opportunity to build a legacy that honors You and impacts generations to come.***

***Your Word declares in Proverbs 13:22 that "A good person leaves an inheritance to their children's children," and I desire to be that person. Help me to walk in wisdom, discipline, and obedience to Your principles so that my life and work reflect Your glory.***

***Father, I surrender my plans to You, knowing that true success is found in aligning my vision with Your Kingdom. Strengthen me to make decisions that create wealth, impact communities, and build a foundation of faith for my family and those connected to me. Remove every distraction, fear, and limiting belief that seeks to hinder my growth, and fill me with divine insight, boldness, and faith to take action.***

***I declare that I am a faithful steward of the resources You have placed in my hands. I honor You with my tithes, offerings, and sowing into Kingdom work, knowing that Malachi 3:10 promises that You will open the floodgates of heaven and pour out blessings beyond measure. As I give, I trust that You will multiply my seed and establish the work of my hands.***

***Let my legacy be one of faith, integrity, and abundance. May my children, spiritual sons and daughters, and those I mentor rise up and call me blessed because I have laid a foundation of wisdom, prosperity, and purpose in You. I declare that my name, my work, and my impact will not be erased but will stand as a testimony of Your faithfulness for generations to come.***

***In Jesus' name, Amen.***

***Legacy Builders Daily Confession***

***I am a Legacy Builder.***
***I walk in divine wisdom, wealth, and purpose.***
***I am anointed to create, steward, and multiply resources.***
***I am disciplined, focused, and committed to building a life that impacts generations.***

***I reject fear, doubt, and scarcity thinking.***
***I embrace abundance, faith, and strategic execution.***
***I sow generously, and I reap abundantly.***
***I am faithful with my tithes and offerings, and the windows of heaven are open over my life.***

***I execute with precision, knowing that my work is not in vain.***
***I am not just making money—I am making a difference.***
***I am not just creating success—I am creating significance.***
***I am not just building wealth—I am building a Kingdom legacy.***

***I declare that my name will be spoken of with honor.***
***My children and their children will benefit from the seeds I sow today.***
***I am a faithful steward, a wise investor, and a bold Kingdom entrepreneur.***

***My legacy will outlive me.***
***My impact will not be erased.***
***I am a builder of wealth, wisdom, and generational blessings.***
***In Jesus' name, Amen.***

# CHAPTER ONE:
# LAYING THE FOUNDATION

***"I am the God of Abraham, and the God of Isaac, and the God of Jacob..." God is not the God of the dead, but of the living." (Matthew 22:32)***

**Legacy Matters...**

How do you want to be known in this life? What mark do you want to leave in the world? How do you envision being remembered long after you have taken your last breath? Believe it or not, these urgent and thought-provoking questions rank among the most important questions everyone must confront as we navigate our journey through life.

## Legacy Matters Key #1

***The formidable power to define your own story lies within you!***

Before delving deeper into the essence of this book, allow me to share a vital life principle that will serve as the underlying theme for this critical work entitled, *Legacy Matters,* and for your life - within you lies the formidable power to define your own story. Here is an important lesson that I had to learn, for me to walk in the truth of who GOD created me to be. Negative circumstances and challenges in your life do not dictate your potential achievements, your success, and the wealth you can accumulate in your lifetime. They do not dictate the course of your life unless you allow them to. It's all up to you. Ultimately, it boils down to your aspirations and desires, how you want your story to be told, and how you want to be known while living and after you leave this life. That, my friend, is legacy.

Meriam-Webster Dictionary defines legacy as *"a gift by will especially of money or other personal property; something transmitted by or received from an ancestor or predecessor or from the past."* However, legacy encompasses far more than these definitions suggest. Legacy is not merely a construct of death. It is a creation of life. Legacy is built while you are living, not when you die. Legacy is shaped by intentional living. It is forged through deliberate, day-to-day living. In essence, legacy is created, one day, one moment, one action, one decision at a time.

Legacy is not just about material wealth and possessions. Legacy is the result of purposeful intention. It transcends the tangible. It encompasses the spirit of our lives. Legacy embodies the essence of our contributions, the resonance of what we leave behind. It is the echo of our actions that lingers after we are gone. Thus, legacy cannot be confined to just material wealth. Legacy is a reflection of who you are.

## Legacy Matters Key #2

***Legacy is an invisible thread that is seen through every aspect of our lives.***

Legacy embodies the purest essence of our existence. It is a mirror reflecting the depth of our character, the values we champion, and the passions that fuel our journey. It captures the essence of our spirit in every choice we make, every relationship we develop, and every challenge we face. Our spiritual legacy transcends the boundaries of time, offering a glimpse into the soul of who we are and the impact of our presence on the world around us. It is not just the memory of your actions, but the warmth of your love, the strength of your convictions, and the vibrancy of your dreams that linger in the hearts and minds of those you touch.

Your legacy is the footprint of your spirit left in the universe. It is the culmination of your laughter, tears, successes, and failures, a picture of your humanity. Each moment of kindness, each act of courage, and each gesture of compassion contributes to this spiritual inheritance, creating a legacy that is uniquely yours. As you navigate the journey of life, your spirit moves through the realms of now and forever, creating a legacy that speaks not just to what you did, but to who you are at your core.

In a nutshell, legacy matters! This is a clarion call to the urgency of legacy creation. Creating a meaningful legacy is a call that cannot wait until your final days of living. It is a process that demands your immediate and focused attention, a commitment to live each day with the end in mind. The power to shape a legacy that transcends time and impacts generations to come rests firmly in your hands. Legacy in its truest form is the deliberate act of intentional living - a tribute to the permanent mark you choose to leave on the earth!

As I ponder the impact of this book, my thoughts turn to two distinct types of readers. The first is the person who seeks practical guidance. The one who says, *"I need to organize my affairs, secure a will, and make sure my insurance is in place."* This reader approaches *Legacy Matters* as a blueprint for action, aiming to alleviate their family from the financial and legal burdens that can accompany the end of life. They are driven by a desire to establish order, to transition from intention to a state of preparedness, making sure that their family obligations are met.

Then there is the second type of reader, the one who, upon reading this book, experiences an awakening. This reader has not yet considered their life from the perspective of legacy. For them, this book acts as a mirror, reflecting not just the practicalities of life's end but the richness and potential of life itself. It is an invitation to embark on a journey of introspection, to incorporate the story of their life into a legacy that goes beyond material concerns.

## Legacy Matters Key #3

***Building your legacy is an act of deliberate intention and desire.***

Both readers are united by a common realization that building your legacy is an act of deliberate intention and desire. How you wish your story to be told and the meaning you instill in your legacy hinges upon the effort you are willing to invest. It encompasses more than just the administrative tasks of legal and financial planning. What we are doing here is creating a life story that has meaning, influence, and lasting importance.

At its core, this book is meant to make you think and act, pushing you to think about not only the practical steps you can take to secure your legacy, but also the bigger picture of how your life affects others. Whether your focus is on the tangible elements of legacy planning or the intangible reflection of your life's meaning, the depth of your engagement determines the richness of the legacy you choose to leave. This book is your guide to understanding that legacy is not just about the end of your life but about every moment that defines it, urging you to live and plan with the end in mind.

The primary goal of this book is to tear down the walls built by excuses. Excuses are a waste of your imaginative power and creative potential. They are a misuse of your imagination. They are a misapplication of your capacity to imagine and to dream. *Legacy Matters* obliterates these justifications for inaction. Why? Because legacy really does matter!

## Legacy Matters Key #4

***Excuses are a misuse of your imagination.***

*Legacy Matters* stands as a clarion call to all, irrespective of background, ethnicity, or economic status. It asserts that your past decisions (or lack thereof), hold no weight against the power of the choices you are yet to make. What is important is the course of action you decide to take once you finish reading the last page of this book. This is an invitation to shift your perspective, to harness your imagination not as a tool for making excuses but as a bridge to actionable, meaningful change. The goal is to eliminate the excuses that bind us all, encouraging each reader to commit to creating a legacy that reflects your innermost values and aspirations. The decisions you have not made until this moment are irrelevant. What matters are the decisions you make after reading this book.

**Living Beyond the Grave**

At the core of our being lies a powerful truth, we are spiritual beings embarking on a human journey. This perspective shifts the understanding of our existence from a purely physical experience to one that is inherently spiritual, where every moment and interaction is layered with a greater purpose. Our bodies are temporary homes for the spirit that lives within us. Our actions, thoughts, and emotions have consequences that extend beyond the physical world. Our true self is not limited by physicality. It transcends time and space.

The spirit man is eternal. This eternal nature of our spirit is what lends such power to the concept of legacy. Unlike physical possessions that can fade, disappear, or deteriorate over time, the spirit carries forward a vibrancy that never wanes. The actions we take, the love we share, the wisdom we impart are expressions of our spirit, all of which impact and change the world in which we live. Therefore, the legacy we create is not just a record of our deeds, but a living, breathing extension of our spirit that continues to influence the world even when we are no longer present physically. It is through our legacy that our spirit finds its voice, continuing to speak, teach, and inspire long after our human experience has ended.

## Legacy Matters Key #5

***You never die!***

The true power of legacy lies in its ability to immortalize the spirit. This is evidence of the lasting influence of our spiritual existence, which persists beyond physical death and resonates throughout history. The spirit of who we are drives us to create and be intentional about legacy. The spirit man lives beyond the grave. The spirit man is proof of the lasting influence of your spiritual existence, an existence that lives on long after you physically die. It continues to play over and over again throughout the ages, generation after generation.

As you create your legacy, you can shape the narrative of your spirit to ensure that the essence of who you are and what you stand for is never forgotten. It is in this act of creation that we find the ultimate expression of our spiritual journey, a journey that transcends the human experience and secures our place in eternity. Through our legacy we affirm the timeless nature of our spirit, demonstrating that while our physical presence may fade, the essence of who we are is everlasting. In other words, you give people a part of who you are while you are living and after you leave this life. In essence, you never die! That is the significance of the spirit man's role in legacy.

**The DNA of GOD**

***"So God created man in his own image, in the image of God created he him; male and female created he them." (Genesis 1:27)***

***"And the LORD God formed man of the dust of the ground, and breathed into his nostrils the breath of life; and man became a living soul." (Genesis 2:7)***

The spirit of man is the DNA of God. The spirit of God dwells within you. At the core of your being, beyond the physical and mental parts that make you who you are, there is a spiritual part that is connected to God, the Creator.

This spiritual DNA is the mark of your divine origin, a blueprint that shapes not just your physical form but your intrinsic nature, values, and purpose. It asserts that every human being possesses a piece of God's divine nature in their soul that ties us profoundly and intricately to both God and one another. This divine DNA is what drives our spiritual endeavors, our search for meaning, and our ability to love and care for others unconditionally.

## Legacy Matters Key #6

***Your view of identity, purpose, and legacy is dramatically transformed when we see ourselves as carriers of God's DNA.***

It elevates the significance of your life's journey from a temporal existence to part of a grand, divine narrative. The spirit man infused with the DNA of God is called to reflect God's character, to steward the creation with wisdom and love, and to cultivate relationships that echo God's relationship with humanity. This perspective instills a sense of responsibility to live in a way that honors this divine inheritance, to nurture our spiritual growth, and to leave a legacy that testifies to the God-like essence within us. It challenges us to live beyond the mundane, to seek alignment with our highest, most divine selves, and to manifest the qualities of our Creator in every aspect of our lives, fulfilling our divine potential and purpose.

The Bible says in Psalm 82:6, *"I have said, Ye are gods; and all of you are children of the most High."* This passage anchors my firm conviction that we are gods. We embody a divine nature that reflects the essence of God. Throughout the Bible, we see the pattern of God demonstrated and the blueprint of divine operation through the actions and teachings of God. God demonstrates for us how gods are supposed to operate. This divine blueprint not only illustrates the operational facets of divinity but also emphasizes the critical importance of creating a lasting legacy. This divine narrative is rich with examples, particularly highlighted in the unique and powerful relationship between God and His son. Their relationship is a vivid illustration of legacy, highlighting the transference of divine values, principles, and missions from one generation to the next.

Furthermore, 1 John 3:2, enriches this discussion by reminding us, "Beloved, now are we the sons of God, and it doth not yet appear what we shall be: but we know that, when he shall appear, we shall be like him; for we shall see him as he is." This passage not only reaffirms our identity as children of God, but it also addresses the transformative journey of aligning with our divine heritage. It hints at the unfolding nature of our divine identity and potential. There is no possible way that God could breathe His Spirit within us and we don't share the same DNA as God.

## Legacy Matters Key #7

***Just because you may not function in your God-ability, does not change who you are.***

Through these scriptural insights, we are encouraged to embrace our godly nature, operate in the manner prescribed by God, and consciously work towards leaving a legacy that reflects our divine lineage. It is through understanding and embodying these principles that we can manifest our role as gods on earth, shaping our legacy in the likeness of the divine example set before us.

In Genesis 17:5, the Amplified Version, God says to Abraham, *"No longer shall your name be Abram (exalted father), But your name shall be Abraham (father of a multitude); For I will make you the father of many nations."* That is the Spirit of God showing us that Abraham no longer lives, but his spirit lives. We are the sons of Abraham; we have been engrafted into the family. The spirit never dies. Until Jesus returns, we will be saying that Abraham is the father of many nations. His seed continues to multiply because of a word spoken over his life. That is the power of legacy.

***"Jesus answered them, Is it not written in your law, I said, Ye are gods? 35 If he called them gods, unto whom the word of God came, and the scripture cannot be broken;" (John 10:34-35)***

Man became a living, speaking God when God breathed into his nostrils, Therefore, we have the ability to walk in the authority that God has given us as gods. Jesus says in John 10:34-35, *"Is it not written in your law, I said, Ye are gods? If he called them gods, unto whom the word of God came, and the scripture cannot be broken."* Just because you may not function in your God-ability, does not change who you are. Did you ever wonder why there are many people who do not function in their God-ability?

1) They do not have a revelation of who they are. They have not been awakened consciously to who God has created and called them to be.

2) They lack awareness of who God is within them and they do not understand their inherent divine potential and capabilities. Without this awareness, it is challenging to tap into and function from a place of higher purpose and power.

3) Fear of failure, doubt in one's abilities, or fear of the unknown can significantly hinder your willingness to step into their full potential. These emotions can create a barrier to exploring and exercising your divine capabilities.

4) Societal norms, cultural expectations, and the voices of authority figures in one's life can sometimes discourage venturing into unknown territories of potential and capabilities, promoting a more conventional path instead.

5) Previous setbacks or traumas can lead to a diminished sense of self-worth or belief in your abilities, making it difficult to fully pursue your divine potential.

6) Without role models, mentors, or guides to help navigate the journey of discovering and utilizing one's divine abilities, many people may struggle to find the path that allows them to flourish.

7) In a world filled with material distractions and instant gratification, it can be challenging to focus on spiritual growth and the development of inherent divine abilities.

8) A disconnection from spiritual practices or beliefs can lead to unawareness or neglect of one's purpose.

Recognizing and overcoming these barriers requires a combination of self-awareness, personal development, spiritual growth, and sometimes guidance from others who have navigated similar journeys. It is imperative to cultivate an environment within and around yourself that nurtures and encourages the exploration and expression of your highest potential.

If you are not aware of who God called you to be, you fail to tap the fullness of your potential and you forfeit the things that God has made available to you. Many people live beneath their God-given ability. They live a life of mediocrity as opposed to the life of abundance that God promised. This lack of awareness leads them to live below the level of excellence and abundance that God has envisioned for them. Instead of stepping into their divine potential, they settle for mediocrity, missing out on the rich, fulfilling life promised by God.

# Legacy Matters Key #8

***True abundance is living a full life filled with purpose, embodying all that God has intended for you to be.***

Abundance is not merely about material possessions. It extends far beyond, to include the fruit of the spirit. True abundance is living a life filled with purpose, embodying all that God has intended for you to be. The joy of the Lord stems from recognizing who God has created and ordained you to be as a living, speaking god. This recognition and fulfillment of our God-ordained roles are what legacy truly entails - living a life that resonates with the depth and breadth of our divine potential.

**The Power of Eternity**

Your spirit man never dies. This truth captures the essence of eternity's power. It goes beyond the idea that life goes on after death and manifests as the ability for our lives to have a lasting influence. Your life has meaning that goes beyond your actual presence on earth. It lives on through the lives and memories of those who come after you. The legacy of those who came before us ensures that our presence remains immortalized on the canvas of life even after we are gone. The achievements and actions of our ancestors continue to inspire and influence us, offering lessons and wisdom that fuel our growth and aspirations. This connection to the past embodies the true spirit of eternity.

Despite never having met many of my ancestors, the essence of their being resonates within me. It is a common experience to be told, *"You act just like your father,"* or to recognize traits within us that align with stories of relatives long passed. These moments highlight how the spirit of our ancestors, their values, and their characteristics ripple through time, impacting generations beyond their own. Such is the power of eternity. It is not merely about the soul's journey after death but about the legacy of spirit that continues to shape the living world long after we are gone. This perspective helps us realize the impact of our actions and the lasting impression we make on the human race, highlighting the importance of living a life that honors this eternal connection.

## Legacy Matters Key #9

***Despite past mistakes or current struggles, your life has immense value and significance.***

Listen… Your legacy matters! This book speaks to those who feel their lives have been irreparably damaged by adversity or negativity to the point where hope for meaning and purpose seems lost. It is especially written for those who are at a crossroads in crafting their legacy, unsure of where to begin, how to take that first step, or even what that step should be towards understanding and creating their legacy. *Legacy Matters* is dedicated to those who have yet to contemplate the legacy they wish to leave behind, aiming to ignite a realization within them - an epiphany of their inherent worth and the potential impact of their existence.

The message at the heart of this book is one of empowerment and revelation. It is a wake-up call to realize that despite past mistakes or current struggles, your life has immense value and significance. The journey outlined in these pages is designed to transform your doubt into confidence, your despair into hope, and your confusion into clarity. It asserts that everyone's life, regardless of its path, is rich with potential to create a meaningful legacy. *Legacy Matters* is for the person who wants to die empty.

## Legacy Matters Key #10

***YOU Matter!***

Through this exploration, I seek to inspire a strong belief in yourself that YES, you can indeed make a difference; YES, your life is worth living; YES, you possess intrinsic value; and YES, YOU MATTER! No matter your past actions or present circumstances, your life is full of meaning waiting to be acknowledged and expressed in the legacy you choose to create.

# CHAPTER TWO:
# YOU MATTER

***"I will praise thee; for I am fearfully and wonderfully made: marvellous are thy works; and that my soul knoweth right well." (Psalm 139:14)***

**Let me begin with a bit more of my story…**

*For the first 53 years of my life, I carried within me a quiet conviction that I was somehow insignificant. I didn't think I mattered. It is amazing what you can do when your dysfunction becomes function and integrates seamlessly into the core of your being, masquerading as normalcy. It wasn't until I decided to go to therapy at the age of 53 that I began to unravel the complexity of my childhood. In those moments of reflection, I came to the realization that I had lived more than half a century doubting my own worth, questioning whether I mattered in the sense I now understand. I have always believed that people loved me, appreciated my contributions, and enjoyed my company, but deep inside I wrestled with the belief of my own significance.*

*Now, this is not a knock against my parents. I believe they did the best they could do with what they knew at the time. Yet, in their efforts, my voice was inadvertently stifled, lost in a sea of expectations and perceived obligations. It took me 54 years to reclaim my voice, to stand firm in my identity and declare that I, indeed, matter. The dysfunction that I once viewed as crippling, became the catalyst for my own transformation. It ignited within me the freedom to be as successful as I wanted to be, fueling my determination to succeed, to be seen, and to carve out a space where I unequivocally mattered.*

*I developed the grit of no quit! My relentless pursuit of achievement and recognition was both a shield and a sword, propelling me to succeed in numerous endeavors in my life, my family, and career. However, amid my triumphs and successes, a revelation emerged from my therapeutic journey: my perception of myself was markedly smaller than how others saw me. It highlighted a pervasive struggle, one that resonates with countless others who feel their value is solely tied to their contributions or the roles they play in the lives of others.*

*Let me be clear. I think I mattered as it relates to what I was giving to others, whether it was support that I offered to the congregation on Sunday mornings as the pastor of my church (as long as you meet people at a point of need, you matter); or the sustenance given to my family (as long as you provide for people, you matter). But I came to realize that my worth is not contingent upon these external validations. This is where many people are trapped, and many contemplate suicide, their sense of self-worth precariously hinged on their last act of service. My story, though deeply personal, echoes a universal cry for recognition of innate value beyond accolades and personal achievements. It is proof of the eternal truth that we all unequivocally matter.*

**The Power of Your Story**

When it comes to intentionally creating your legacy, your story matters. The deliberate construction of your legacy is contingent upon the significance of your story. Let me be very clear. Your story holds significance. There is power in your story. Why? Your story matters. It is fundamental to the legacy you build. It is a narrative that is uniquely yours. It is the way you view life your life, not merely a story as remembered by others.

## Legacy Matters Key #11

***Your narrative lays the foundation for your legacy.***

Understanding your story and fully embracing it - the highs, the lows, the twists and turns, the setbacks and unexpected developments - is a vital component of building your legacy. It makes the difference in how you interpret and understand your path. Your narrative lays the foundation for your legacy. Therefore, you need to have a solid understanding of your story and fully embrace it.

Your story is your perception. It is your view. It is your vantage point. What makes your story powerful, relevant and important is how you see it, not how others tell it. Your experiences are personal. However, if you do not control the narrative, once you have departed from this life, people will attempt to piece together their knowledge based on the parts of your life they have witnessed or heard about. How you see your story is your narrative. Telling it your way offers the chance to share your perspective infused with your own thoughts, feelings, and viewpoints. This type of control over your story is powerful. It allows you to clarify misunderstandings and present a more complex, true-to-life version of YOU that goes beyond everyday interactions or fleeting moments.

Many of us struggle with being fully understood, walking the fine line between being open and maintaining privacy, all while searching for a space to fully express and reveal our true selves. The truth is, while we are living and after we leave this life, everyone has and will have their perception of our stories, as they only see tidbits and hear sound bites of it. However, our lives are often far more complicated than what people get to see on a daily basis.

## Legacy Matters Key #12

***Transforming the narrative begins with a genuine recognition of where you currently stand, which calls for introspection and deep reflection.***

I am very careful to correct people when they say they know me - *You don't know me. You know of me.* There are very few people who know me, and even they do not really know me. Most of us are not transparent enough with our lives or have not found a place safe enough to be able to have people know us in our very vulnerable states. Yet, transforming the narrative begins with a genuine recognition of where you currently stand, which calls for introspection and deep reflection. You have to first know your story. It is about acknowledging your journey, digging into the origins of your values, beliefs, and dreams and understanding how they have been shaped by your experiences and surroundings.

Keep in mind, it is possible that this level of introspection may surface ideas and beliefs that do not connect with who you are at the present time. Maybe you have been true to something that really hasn't been true to you. Maybe you have been true to something that is really not you. That is the power of introspection. If you are not careful, you might perpetuate something from a legacy standpoint that really is not you but was given to you out of someone else's pain or misunderstanding of their own story. If you choose not to take this deep dive into personal reflection and introspection, you could very well be perpetuating a false narrative of who you are or tolerating something that you are dissatisfied with but with which you have learned to live.

There are many things that we do because of learned behaviors, so much so that we learn to be satisfied with our dissatisfaction because that is all we know; and it became the norm. That can be a travesty. In this process, you will find that there are people that you love, respect and honor, but they may not have been the best role models for *your* life. Listen, there are no perfect people, but there are certain aspects of my life that I choose not to be a part of my story.

Personal reflection and introspection offer a moment to identify and let go of inherited stories or behaviors that clash with your true self, paving the way to create a narrative that genuinely reflects who you are and who you want to be. It is a decision to ensure your legacy is not a reflection of other people's pain or misconceptions, but a story that is authentically yours. As you create your narrative, you are not only rejecting what does not serve you but also embracing and affirming your identity, values, and ambitions. This ensures that your legacy accurately represents you, making it a true reflection of the unique and powerful person you are.

## Legacy Matters Key #13

***Within your story is the power to shape not just your legacy but also how you understand and navigate your journey.***

Let me share another piece of my story to illustrate just how powerful stories are in creating our legacy. By sharing fragments of my own legacy journey, I hope to highlight how important it is to dig deep within to reflect on who you are and where you are going in crafting your legacy. *I do not want to instruct you on how to bake a cake without ever having baked one myself.* I want to show you the real deal - the trials and the triumphs, and how these moments shape us; then invite you to look within to explore your own experiences and how they contribute to the legacy you want to leave. This is about authenticity, about being true to yourself and your story, and recognizing that within your story is the power to shape not just your legacy but also how you understand and navigate your journey.

*My initial memories of my childhood are tainted with the absence of my biological father and the echo of his unfulfilled promises. These early experiences are vividly etched in my mind, marking the beginning of my life's narrative. However, the entrance of a significant figure, my stepfather (though we never labeled him as such), marked a pivotal turn in my story. My stepfather stepped into the void left by my biological father, taking on a role of guidance and support that profoundly influenced my development. This dual effect, which encompassed both the anguish of being abandoned and the warmth of being accepted, was the driving force behind my determination and my drive to succeed.*

*My journey led to reconciling with my biological father and leading him to Christ. Through our reunion, he was able to undergo a personal transformation and gain an awareness of God's love. He told me that he now understands the love of God through my loving him despite his flaws. Today, he is saved, loves God and is committed to the things of God as a result of my love walk with him. This highlights the fundamental truth that our actions and connections with people have the power to heal wounds, bridge gaps, and overcome past hurts and broken promises.*

## Legacy Matters Key #14

***Legacy is not just about the mark we leave on others but about recognizing our worth and the unique story we each have to tell.***

Reflecting on these personal experiences brings to mind a poignant biblical query that Jesus said, "Who do you say that I am?" This question challenges the common tendency to define ourselves by our professions or achievements. Yet, who we really are transcends what we do. Sharing this part of my life underscores the reality that transformation and healing are within reach, offering a lived experience rather than theory.

Legacy is not just about the mark we leave on others but about recognizing our worth and the unique story we each have to tell. Legacy is not an external construct created for other people; it is about YOU - your life and how you choose to craft your story. It is your life, your legacy, your blueprint. At the end of the day, you are the architect of your story. You are the star. You are the leading actor. So, YOU matter!

**Legacy Matters Exercise**

*Your turn. Take a moment and begin to start crafting your story. Reflect on your values and beliefs, reflect on your early influences, reflect on your strengths and weaknesses, reflect on your skills, passions, interests, and goals. Why? Because you matter!*

Who were the most influential people in your childhood and why?

What are your earliest memories?

What aspects of your life do you want to use to craft your legacy?

List your skills, passions, interests, and goals.

What are your dreams and aspirations?

**It's About You!**

Many people believe that legacy is about leaving something for others. If they don't have something "to leave" for other people (tangible assets), they feel they don't have a legacy. Somewhere in their mind they feel that they don't matter. You matter just because you were born. Your significance was inherent from the moment of your birth. You matter because you are a deliberate creation of God placed within your specific family by divine design. You have a unique, divine purpose and assignment for this life. You may not think of it as an assignment. You may think of it as a job or something that you do. But in the big picture, it is something that God has assigned you to do. It is a specific role that only you are equipped to fulfill.

Think about it. You made it here against incredible odds right from the start. Out of the countless sperm cells to make their way to a fertilized egg, you made it. That alone says you are here for a reason. You matter! Your life is not the sum of what you give to others. The sum of your life is what you give to yourself. Some people may say that is selfish, but it is not. It is what you give to yourself.

# Legacy Matters Key #15

***The focus of legacy is YOU, emphasizing your own significance.***

Focusing on your own growth and your own happiness is not selfish. Actually, it is the opposite. By investing in yourself and becoming the best version of YOU, you are setting the stage to make a difference in your family, your community, and the world. You must recognize the power of what you give to you so that you can give to others. It is from this place of self-care and understanding that you can effectively and powerfully touch the lives of others, showing the divine connection between taking care of yourself and meaningfully contributing to the world around you.

Another common misconception is that legacy pertains solely to its impact on other people, overlooking that at its core legacy is personal. It is about the one who is leaving the legacy. It is about the life you have lived, the wisdom you have gathered, and the stories that only you can tell. The focus of legacy is YOU, emphasizing *your* own significance.

Many people feel like they don't matter. Many are plagued by feelings of insignificance, often evaluating their worth based on material achievements or contributions. But here is a little reminder. Your legacy is a celebration of you being you, bringing something special to the world's table that no one else can. It is easy to forget this, especially when you are caught up in doing for others, whether that is parenting, helping out in the community, caregiving, or in my case, pastoring a congregation of people. Sometimes we lose ourselves in these roles.

The trap of always putting others first can mean you live your life more for "them" and less for you, missing out on appreciating your own life. Oftentimes, no matter how much you give, it is never enough. People are always looking for what's next. It is disheartening to think that you become less significant to people when you "run out" of things to give. If you are not careful, you can spend your whole life giving to others that you forget to enjoy the life that you live because you have always made it about other people. ***Legacy is not just about what you leave behind but about the essence of who you are!***

# Legacy Matters Key #16

***It is vital for your value to be recognized and acknowledged.***

You are the heart of your legacy. It is vital for your value to be recognized and acknowledged. Your value does not change based on life's ups and downs. You matter beyond what you can offer. Understanding this truth is not just about changing how you view things; it is about embracing the truth that you, your being, and your story are irreplaceable gifts to the world. You were fearfully and wonderfully made by God. It is paramount for people to recognize your value.

There is this thing that happens to a lot of us who have big hearts – we are always giving, giving, giving, pouring out kindness, support, whatever we can, without ever thinking of getting anything back. Most givers do not know how to receive. It is easy to feel like nobody really sees how much you do, or feel the vibe that you are only as good as the help you offer. Sometimes we don't hear enough that we matter, falling into a trap that can lead us to mistakenly believe that our significance is merely a function of our generosity.

The challenge is many people disregard that they matter. They place other people's values above their own and above themselves. They see other people as more valuable or more deserving, which is the furthest thing from the truth. You are a "Designer's original" (the Designer being God), and you matter. Your past does not matter. It does not matter what other people might think about you. It does not matter what you may have thought about yourself. You, yourself, must understand that you matter, that you are important to God, and that you are valuable. The real value of legacy is that in the end, no matter what you leave, you are giving YOU. YOU matter, and YOU must make sure that others know that YOU MATTER.

**A Designer's Original**

You have to embrace the self-realization that your life is worth living. Take a moment and speak these words out of your mouth, *"My life is worth living."* If you are looking back over your life wondering about the footprints you have left in your family, community and the world, thinking that the daily grind was all there was to your story and to your legacy, I want you to think again. Let me share something vital about your legacy. You are a Designer's original, nothing short of a masterpiece that was intricately designed with a purpose that only you can fulfill.

# Legacy Matters Key #17

***Recognize and acknowledge that your life is worth something and you are not an afterthought.***

Before God formed you and placed you in your mother's womb, He knew you, all of your fears, your faults, your priorities, your failures. Yet you were chosen and lovingly created. God (working as the Potter) used all of that to bring you to this crescendo in life where you reflect upon your life and begin to put the pieces together so that you can pass it on to the next generation. You may have had some pitstops, you may have had some pitfalls, you may have had some detours and disappointments, but remember, the essence of a fulfilling life lies not in perfection but in understanding and embracing your value and purpose.

Recognize and acknowledge that that your life is worth something and that you are not an afterthought. You were a thought within "heaven's corridor," the mind of God. You may not have always gotten it right, but as long as you have breath in your body, you still have a chance to make it right. God is a God of another chance - not a first, second, or third chance, but *another* chance. He works with grace, offering endless opportunities for renewal and redemption. That is the value in understanding the way God sees you. God uses ordinary people to do extraordinary things. This understanding lifts the weight of condemnation, opening the doors to living fully in the light of God's love. As you embrace this divine truth about yourself, you will begin to understand the depth and significance of your legacy.

**You Are Valuable**

***"And be not conformed to this world: but be ye transformed by the renewing of your mind, that ye may prove what is good, and acceptable, and perfect, will of God." (Romans 12:2)***

No matter where you come from, your social standing, or what you have accomplished in this life, everyone has this deep, inherent worth. It is like this undeniable value that is part of who we are. A lot of what shapes our value is not about us. It is about where we have been, how we were raised, and the lessons and beliefs that have been instilled in us along the way.

## Legacy Matters Key #18

***Renewing your mind requires consistent and deliberate thoughts, actions and conversations.***

For instance, certain races of people have a belief that they are superior to other races, a notion deeply ingrained from teachings sometimes subtly passed down from generation to generation. In many cases, they have been taught that they are better. This belief, rooted in the mere fact of their skin color, is an example of how perceived inherent value can be shaped by the environment, family values, upbringing, and the narratives shared within families and communities. Even those who have much less have been taught that they are better because of the color of their skin. This is a learned value that has been taught over time.

Romans 12:2 says that we are transformed by the renewing of our minds. If you want to know your value and your worth and build a legacy around who you really are (and not who the world dictates you are), you have to renew your mind. But it does not happen overnight. It takes guarding your heart. How do you do that? Renewing your mind requires consistent and deliberate thoughts, actions and conversations. You have to be careful about the words you let into your spirit and the people you give the power to influence you. Then the process of reprogramming begins. Once you start this process, you begin the journey of rethinking how you see everything.

For many of us in the Black community, this is a familiar path. We have had to work on changing our mindset because of the systemic racism and inequalities we face daily. However, it is not just about racism, though that is a big part of it, but the inequalities we experience as a people. For many generations, Black people thought they did not matter just because of the color of their skin. Over the years, as a people, we have had to renew our minds and teach ourselves that we do matter. That has been a huge shift for many of us, moving from feeling insignificant to knowing our worth.

**Allow me to share a bit more of my story to highlight this point…**

Navigating life with my five-year-old granddaughter (at the time of writing this book), has opened my eyes to the realities she is beginning to face in a world still grappling with issues of equality and racism. At her private school where she is among a small number of Black students, she is already encountering situations that challenge her self-worth. She has to qualify as a five-year-old that she has value and that she, in fact, does matter. It is heart-wrenching to think that at such a young age she has to affirm her own importance in a space where she should feel safe and cherished.

*My family made it our mission to reinforce that she matters. We constantly instill in her affirmations of her value and remind her daily that she is a queen born with an undeniable significance, because we know who we are. But trying to shield her from the less-than-positive energy that might seep into her young spirit from her surroundings is a sobering task.*

*I'll never forget how she wanted to share with her teacher a picture of herself standing next to our Christmas tree at home. In her young mind, I believe she wanted to share the photo with her teacher as a way of qualifying that she is not less than. It was her way of asserting her equality, a silent but powerful statement.*

This serves as a vivid reminder that the journey to self-worth starts at an early age. It is important that you renew your mind and begin to see yourself in light of who God has created you to be. Embracing this divine viewpoint will help you stand firm in your unique value, regardless of external challenges.

## Legacy Matters Key #19

***Renewing your mind and grasping the depth of your God-given identity is a lifelong process.***

As believers, we must constantly renew our minds, refreshing our perspectives, a journey I am personally navigating, and truth be told, it is a process. It is not like you hit the finish line and everything is suddenly set in stone. Renewing your mind and grasping the depth of your God-given identity is a lifelong process. The world around us, with all its systems and standards, seems almost engineered to make people feel inadequate, whether it's about not owning the latest luxury items, living a certain lifestyle, or fitting into a particular mold. But here is the thing: none of that stuff defines you! None of those things make you who you are. What makes you who you are is knowing who you are, whose you are, and understanding your place as a child of the Most High God. That is the core of who we are.

For anyone who is reading this and feeling that "a-ha moment," know this: these moments of clarity should not be one-off moments. It is about continuously seeking those revelations, putting yourself in environments that reflect the way God views you. It is an ongoing process of discovery, a path to seeing ourselves through the lens of God.

**Heaven On Earth**

When you see yourself through the lens of God, you begin to see who God created you to be and all that He purposed for you to have and to do. Missing out on the incredible opportunities God has given us feels like we are not only shortchanging ourselves but also those we are meant to uplift and lead. Let me let you in on a powerful truth. You can experience heaven on earth! You do not have to wait until you die to experience heaven if you live intentionally and purposefully, and if you put certain things in place for your legacy to have that heaven on earth experience. However, you have to be intentional about your legacy.

Do you know what God has made available to you? Do you know the legacy He destined you to leave? If you answered any of these questions in the negative, it means that you could be cheating not only yourself, but generations to come, out of your God-ordained inheritance just because you refuse to access all that is available to you while you are living. When you think about it in the context of what God has made available for us, consider what you possibly leave, what you could possibly cheat yourself out of, whether spiritually, mentally, or materially, just because you did not take advantage of what God made available to you. When we consider the abundance laid before us, it becomes essential to deeply consider the implications of not fully embracing these gifts. This reflection is not just about personal losses but also about what we fail to contribute to the lives of our loved ones, family, and community.

# Legacy Matters Key #20

***You can experience heaven on earth!***

Understanding the value of experiencing heaven on earth is a game-changer in creating your legacy. It requires a shift in perspective, inviting us to understand the importance of living deliberately and with purpose, and begin to experience heaven right here in the present. This mindset urges us not only to think about the legacy we will leave behind but to actively nurture and enjoy those divine aspects of life right now. Adopting this way of living not only makes our lives richer, but it also ensures we hand down a legacy brimming with fulfilled potential and heavenly experiences, rather than simply passing on unfulfilled dreams for others to decipher.

You matter right now. Your thoughts, feelings, and actions are significant in this very moment. How you choose to live today is part of the legacy you are building. Remember, it is not just about what you leave *for* people, but what you leave *in* people.

**Break the Mold!**

As you work through this chapter and realize that YOU MATTER, begin to disengage from self-imposed limitations. What are self-imposed limitations? They are limitations we place on ourselves based on our personal experiences. They are invisible barriers we set that are rooted in our personal history and environment. Self-imposed limitations are based on the environment, historical context, and what we were told we could have based on the communities in which we were raised. They are the ceilings we are told exist, shaped by the stories and roles presented to us. Self-imposed limitations severely limit our potential, holding us back from fulfilling the expansive vision God has for our lives.

Regardless of who you are, we all encounter self-imposed limitations at some point. Breaking free from them is essential. I've been there myself.

# Legacy Matters Key #21

***Self-imposed limitations stifle you from being and becoming all that God says that you can be.***

*Growing up, I was encouraged by my mother's words that I could achieve anything, hearing, "You can be a fireman, you can be a police officer. You can be the president of the United States. You can be..." The problem is we didn't see people that looked like us being those things. I grew up hearing this, but there were still self-imposed limitations based on my environment and community. Like many in my generation, the lack of visible role models resembling me in the ambitions I was encouraged to pursue created an invisible boundary. It became a detriment because although I heard my family members say that I could be a certain thing, I did not see anyone being what they were telling me I could be. Despite being told I could reach any height, the absence of tangible examples in my immediate world cast a shadow of doubt.*

*My legacy journey has been about shattering these limitations, venturing into territories uncharted by anyone in my family. I am the first to break into a space that did not exist for me based on my environment and community. I chose to embark on a path to become something beyond the precedents set by my environment and community, proving that your starting point doesn't have to dictate where you can go.*

# Legacy Matters Key #22

***Self-imposed limitations are a detriment to your destiny.***

The disconnect between aspirations and reality is a roadblock to realizing your destiny. The absence of visible examples does not mean achieving your dreams is impossible. Just because you don't know something exists, or a career exists, or entrepreneurial possibilities exist for you, does not mean they don't exist. However, self-imposed limitations will stop you from pursuing those opportunities. Self-imposed limitations will stifle you from being and becoming all that God says that you can be.

# CHAPTER THREE:
# LEGACY MATTERS

***"Legacy is not leaving something for people. It's leaving something in people." (Peter Strobel)***

**How Will Your Story End?**

Legacy is more than a memory. It is the lasting imprint one leaves on the world. It echoes a life lived with purpose, passion and intention. Legacy is your life, how people view and see your life in living as well as after death. How do you want to be remembered? What mark do you want to leave in this world both during your lifetime and after you leave this life?

When I think about my legacy, it is not merely about milestones or recognition. It is deeper than that. It is about the principles I stand for, the people whose lives I have made better, the financial stability and economic impact that I am working to firmly establish, and the meaningful differences I have made and still make in my family and community.

## Legacy Matters Key #23

***Life needs to be lived on purpose and in purpose.***

How does your family see you? Are people's lives better because you were a part of their community? Thinking about how you want your story to end will cause you to do everything with intention to make sure that your story ends the way that you want it to end. It is like a writer writing a story. The writer knows how they want the story to end. The question is the "stuff" in the middle. That is where the intention lives. What happens in the middle helps us achieve the ending that we desire.

What are you doing to be remembered? Again, life should be lived on purpose and in purpose. If you are going to live on purpose and in purpose, then you have to be purposeful, intentional and methodical. You must develop the discipline to go the distance. You have to live a disciplined life to ensure that you get the desired outcome. For me, it has been a game-changer in steering my life's direction. Living on purpose and in purpose will determine how your life will ultimately end. How intentional are you about the things that you put in place to ensure that what you believe to be your ending happens. You have to purposefully set up routines and safeguards to ensure that the future you dreamt comes to pass.

Legacy is about making a meaningful contribution that outlasts your life and continues to influence and inspire others. It is a reflection of your life work and the imprint you leave on the world and others. Legacy is not a new concept. We see the thread of legacy throughout the Bible. God is a God of legacy.

Matthew 22:32 says, *"I am the God of Abraham, and the God of Isaac, and the God of Jacob? God is not the God of the dead, but of the living."* Legacy is empowering, educational and enlightening. Legacy is exciting! Building your legacy is an exciting journey when you know that your life matters. When you leave this life, your legacy will depict that you matter because of how you educated, empowered and enlightened, and eliminated the stress and struggle of those in your family and immediate community.

## Legacy Matters Key #24

***Creating a rich, lasting and impactful legacy can eliminate the burdens and obstacles that your family may have faced if it were not for your influence.***

Creating a powerful legacy requires giving everything you can (methods, morality, money, mentality and message) to alleviate the stress, struggles, hardships and challenges faced by those in your immediate circle and anyone you have impacted in any manner.

Legacy encompasses 5 things. Your methods, morality, money, mentality and message. **Methods** deal with the process; **Morality** deals with righteous living as a believer, doing things God's way; **Money** gives you the ability to have choices; **Mentality** deals with having the mental toughness and tenacity it takes to manage everything; and the **message** is clear, everything is done on purpose and in purpose. You do not get here by accident. These are the ingredients to living a fulfilled life, one that is purposefully lived and emptied.

# Legacy Matters Key #25

***Leave nothing to chance.***

My life is guided by a saying that emphasizes the need for being proactive and not relying on luck - leave nothing to chance. You are not going to accidentally leave the legacy that you desire to leave. You are not going to accidentally get out of debt. You are not going to accidentally be financially fit. You are not going to accidentally live a moral lifestyle. You have to be very structured and systematic - again, living life on purpose and in purpose.

My goal is to live debt-free and live a righteous life. Yet, neither of these can be achieved without structure and a system. It does not happen by osmosis. It happens because I make conscious choices and decisions that move me towards my desired goal.

Legacy is a spirit. The spirit of legacy lives beyond what you may see on the outside. It is when you perceive legacy from within an individual that you truly understand that legacy is spirit. Once you develop the mentality and the spirit of legacy, it lives beyond the physical to something that endures forever, because legacy lives beyond things.

There have been many successful people who felt like they made it in life, yet they may not have left the legacy they desired. Making a positive impact on others does contribute to legacy, but it does not necessarily mean there were deliberate efforts and actions towards building a specific legacy. Many people make a difference in the lives of others without really focusing on the kind of legacy they wish to leave behind. You leave a message when you make other people's lives better. Making people's lives better matters. Doing good for others matters. However, just because someone is successful does not mean that they will create the legacy they desire. You need to be intentional about your legacy.

Everyone contributes in some way to improving the lives of others, whether we mean to or not. Much of the good that we do happens without even trying. However, to equate legacy solely with the positive influence we have on people is simplistic. You can learn a valuable lesson from the meanest, ungrateful, and least admirable person you know. You can discover what kind of person you don't want to be. Defining legacy just as the mark we leave on others only scratches the surface of its depth.

***"A good man leaveth an inheritance to his children's children:" (Proverbs 13:22)***

Legacy is not just about you. It includes your family, stretching from those closest to you to the broader branches of your family tree. It is also deeply intertwined with your faith, reflecting what you stand for and the beliefs that are important to you. Moreover, legacy is about your battles - the causes and principles you have championed throughout your life. Finally, legacy is about your financial well-being, how you manage the resources God entrusted to you, and what you are able to pass on after you leave this life.

The journey of building a legacy for your children starts the moment they enter the world. Parents often dream about who their children will grow up to be and then dedicate themselves to shaping that future. Every decision, every action we take as parents is an investment in their future. Why? Future matters.

## Legacy Matters Key #26

***Start where you are.***

The moment we welcome our children, our entire mindset shifts. It starts with the overwhelming happiness of bringing a child into the world. Soon after the initial burst of joy, many of us begin planning for the future, often without realizing it. Drawing from our own life lessons we think about what we hope they will not become, and then we start dreaming about what we desire for them to become. From then on, a big part of our lives is dedicated to nurturing them, guiding them to grow into the best possible version of themselves. This version is intricately connected to our own ideas and goals for what we think they will develop into in the future.

There is a common misconception that creating a legacy is about having a lot of money. But honestly, it is about starting from wherever you are right now. That's right… START WHERE YOU ARE! It starts with the revelation that your legacy matters. It starts with understanding that your life is legacy, and legacy is your life. When that understanding clicks, you begin to see things differently, realizing the importance of actively shaping your legacy from any starting point. If all you own is the clothes on your back, start there.

Here is a short scenario:

**Estate Attorney:** Who do you want your clothes to go to?

**You:**I want everything I own to be given to Goodwill to be a blessing to someone in need.

It is a reminder that whatever you have accumulated in life, you have the power to decide its final destination. You can take control of your story, choosing how you want your final chapter to conclude and leaving a narrative that reflects your wishes and values. That might sound small, but it is a way to grasp the broader picture - living life with the conviction that what you do and have matters.

## Legacy Matters Key #27

***Legacy begins when you awaken to the realization that your life stretches beyond the routine of daily life.***

Everyone has the capacity to do this, no matter where you are in life. Many people think they have plenty of time on their hands, especially young adults. But the truth is, thinking about legacy is not a task reserved for middle age or later years. Legacy begins when you awaken to the realization that your life stretches beyond the routine of daily life. Yet, how you live each day contributes to the legacy you are building. Some may say, *"Man, you're talking about legacy? I'm just trying to get by day-to-day."* But here is the kicker: living day-to-day is creating your legacy. Regardless of your financial standing, every choice you make, every moment of your day is a piece of your legacy being etched into time. The important component to focus on is narrating your story and making every day count.

Even if you live from paycheck to paycheck and continuously struggle to make ends meet, you must share your story in a way that speaks to others. Sometimes it might just be about sharing what not to do, lessons learned the hard way. If you feel like you missed your moment or think it is too late for change, remember it is NEVER too late. Whatever message of hope or encouragement you extend to someone else in your shoes, that same message applies to you. It is never too late to make a difference, to rewrite your story in a way that not only changes your path but also lights the way for others.

What's Love Got To Do With It?

***"For God so loved the world, that he gave his only begotten Son, that whosoever believeth in him should not perish, but have everlasting life." (John 3:16)***

You might wonder, what does love have to do with legacy? Well, navigating this journey of life is a love walk. Love has everything to do with it. Love is at the core of it all. Love seeks to always give the advantage. Love is at the heart of everything, especially when it comes to legacy. Love inherently aims to uplift others. As believers, our foundational legacy is rooted in the act of love. God loved the world so much that He gave His only Son. That is the epitome of legacy.

# Legacy Matters Key #28

***Love seeks to always give the advantage.***

Love's nature is to offer a hand up, to generously give. Love and legacy are inseparable. It would be a crime, a shame, and an indictment on those of us who profess to love our work, our divine mission, and the communities we serve, to neglect being deliberate about the legacy we create and leave. It's not just about the impact we have after we are gone. It is about the legacy we leave while living.

Love has everything to do with it. When you love someone, your instinct is to give them a leg up. We want to temper the conditions that give them the advantage. It is about wanting the best for the people we love, for the communities we are a part of, and fulfilling the purpose God has assigned to us, which to spread love and make the world a better place. Striving to leave a legacy entails doing our best to leave a good name, live a fulfilling life, give all we have to give, and die empty. Love seeks to be the greatest giver and the bigger blesser.

Dr. Martin Luther King Jr., the esteemed civil rights activist and freedom fighter, lost his life in the name of love. His legacy speaks of his love for people and the idea of justice for all people, regardless of their race, creed or color. He had a tremendous impact on the civil rights movement. However, I often question the impact of the commemorations on his legacy. His love ran so deep that he lost his life fighting for the freedom of others. Yet, it seems like we only focus on Dr. King's robust legacy once a year - during the celebrations in his honor.

The question remains, is the essence of who he was and what he contributed to this world reflected in his legacy? Are the marches and memorials truly reflective of his contributions, or do they risk becoming annual rituals that do not fully align with his principles, beliefs and what he fought for?

To me, it feels like Dr. King's legacy is more about memorialization than actualization, especially for the younger generation. He is recognized as a pivotal figure of the civil rights movement, but probing deeper into what he truly stood for might reveal gaps in understanding. While his commitment to nonviolence is widely acknowledged, I cannot help but feel that with each passing generation, a bit of the essence of what he fought for is diluted. His legacy, though solidly established, seems to lose a bit of its vibrancy and relevance over time. It feels like we only engage with Dr. King's legacy once a year, during the annual celebrations in his honor. We continue to hold marches, memorial events, oratory programs, "I Have A Dream" speech reiterations, and the like, but how do these traditions events and memorials serve his legacy? What message are we sending about the depth and breadth of his impact through these commemorations?

Of course, the world knows that he led the nonviolence movement, but I believe with every generation his legacy is diluted. This gradual dilution of meaning is not just about time passing. It is more about how his legacy is preserved and presented. Despite the speeches and marches commemorated in his honor, it seems like these actions do not spark significant change, nor do they engage today's youth in a meaningful way. Even though Dr. King's legacy is solidified in the books of history, we seem to struggle with making his legacy resonate with the current times and challenges we face.

We seem to get caught up in commemorating what Dr. King achieved, rather than engaging with how his actions continue to influence us now. Year after year, we memorialize the man, yet not really building on what he has done and moving that vision forward. So, it begs the question: what exactly is his legacy? At some point, there will be a generation who is going to say, "Okay, who cares?" This attitude might shock those who have lived closer to his era and feel a deeper connection to his impact. Yet, this disconnect raises a valid point about the importance of making historical legacies relevant and inspiring to today's youth.

Has his legacy become just another memorial of one of our great heroes? Was his dying in vain? Will his underlying love for people be overshadowed by a lack of passion for the cause for which he died? The questions I pose around Dr. King's legacy emphasize the importance of assuming responsibility for shaping your own story, ensuring that each action and choice you make is a purposeful contribution to the life you live. Did Dr. King consciously design his legacy, or was his journey cut short before he could do so?

Considering his unexpected departure, did Dr. King's family have to piece together his legacy from the actions and words he left behind, crafting a narrative from which future generations draw inspiration and direction? This highlights the importance of intentionality in legacy-building and the role of loved ones in preserving and interpreting the legacy of those who die prematurely.

## Legacy Matters Key #29

***It is important to externalize and implement your legacy vision so that it does not remain solely in your mind.***

Remember, love always seeks to give the advantage. Keeping your legacy merely as thoughts and plans locked away in your mind is a risk. Should you pass away with those intentions still inside, your legacy might fade away with you, leaving room for others to craft their interpretations of who you were, what you aimed to achieve, and the impact you hoped to make. Essentially, your legacy could be overshadowed by narratives that do not fully capture your life and intentions. It is important to externalize and implement your legacy vision so that it does not remain solely in your mind.

This work is not easy, but it can be accomplished. You have to be willing to face your failures, your highs and your lows. You have to be willing to acknowledge your strengths and your weaknesses. You have to be open to doing a full introspection of your life and being okay with what you find. You have to be willing to deal with the good, the bad, and the ugly in every area of your life, be it your finances, family, or faith.

Many people shy away from actively shaping their legacy due to the effort required. However, the work is rewarding once you go through the process. That is what legacy is all about – the process. Embarking on this journey, despite its demands, proves to be immensely fulfilling. Legacy is fundamentally about engaging with this process and embracing the work involved. This is about your life and the essence of why you are here. Dedicating yourself to this endeavor is undoubtedly worth every bit of the effort.

***The ultimate measure of a man is not where he stands in moments of comfort and convenience, but where he stands at times of challenge and controversy.***

***~Dr. Martin Luther King, Jr.***

# Legacy Matters Key #30

***It is imperative to understand your WHY.***

A major part of creating our legacy is understanding our why. As I started to intentionally create my legacy, I had to ask myself, "what" is my why? In my life in general, "where" is my why? Can my why be identified in my family? Can my why be identified in my business? Can my why be identified in my community contributions? Can my why be identified in church and the good that I have done in serving the people of God?

Why do we pour so much effort into our work? Why have we made so many sacrifices? Why have we dedicated ourselves to serving our community, our family, and fulfilling what we see as our divine purpose? Reflecting on these questions of service and sacrifice illuminates the purpose of our lives and shapes the legacy we aim to create. This contemplation has led me to consider the importance of creating my legacy, ensuring that the values I cherish and the work I have done endure beyond our time.

It is imperative to understand your WHY. As you begin to think about your why, it puts things in perspective for you as to the meaning of your life and the legacy you ultimately want to leave. I had to contemplate some important questions. Does my family really understand my WHY? Have they fully bought into my WHY? Will I just be another person where the people say, "He was a good pastor," without understanding the magnitude and depth of my assignment? What lives have I touched that I will never know that I touched? It is not just the lives of the people you touch, but it is the lives they have touched because you touched them.

Allow me to share a bit more of my story and what I discovered about me as I walked this journey of creating my own legacy.

*My name, Amos, means burden bearer. I believe I was born to be a difference maker. For over two decades, my mission has been to help bridge the wealth gap, empowering and educating people, particularly people of color, about how to get out of debt, how to finance their dreams, how to build wealth, and how to become a part of the top one percent of the world. I am a prophet born to bring deliverance to people's lives in whatever area they are bound. I believe I am meant to be this beacon of hope for anyone caught in any kind of tough spot, but my focus is helping people become financially free. I see myself as a modern-day Moses here to lead people out of whatever is keeping them from reaching their full potential in life and living out their real purpose.*

*People are often their own biggest barriers, held back by low self-esteem or the shadows of their past mistakes. I believe that I was born for those individuals. Many people are held captive to the mistakes of their past. I've had to overcome my own personal mistakes and still was able to be successful. Beyond personal obstacles, there are generational curses and financial entanglements that bind us, keeping us from understanding the pathways to freedom.*

*I am living proof that you do not have to be subject to the generational curses that plague your family. Many people are held captive to financial bondage, not knowing how to get out of their situation. My background in business, psychology, theology, and counseling equips me to address the financial, psychological and emotional chains that hold people back. With this knowledge, I aim to unlock their potential, instilling the belief in limitless possibilities through intentional actions and purpose-driven living.*

*This approach, while methodical and sometimes at odds with spontaneous fun, underscores every aspect of my efforts to make a significant, meaningful impact. I believe I have the keys that unlock those things that help free people up to believe again, to become what God has purposed them to be, and to know that anything is possible. I am a very intentional person. So, everything that I do is with a plan and a purpose. This approach means I am not always the life of the party when it comes to my family, but it is how I know I can make a real, lasting difference. My perspective is we can have fun, but let's be intentional so that we can have the fun that we want to have.*

*Nonetheless, it emphasizes my efforts to have a substantial and meaningful impact in this life.*

What you just read about me was the summary of my why. It is an integral part of the legacy building process. It may seem simple, but it is part of getting your affairs in order. It is a process, but it is well worth it. Often, it is thefundamental steps that many people overlook or delay.

# CHAPTER Four:
# HEART MATTERS

***"Delight yourself also in the Lord, and He will give you the desires and secret petitions of your heart." (Psalm 37:4)***

**It's A Heart Thing**

Legacy is a heart matter. It reflects those things we desire to leave behind for our families, loved ones, communities and the world. It also includes the emotional and spiritual gifts we choose to share. It is the love, the wisdom, and the values we want to leave for this world and those we hold close to our hearts. In a nutshell, legacy reflects what matters most to us, the things that we cherish, and hope people will remember about us or remember us for.

Because of the busyness of life and the day-to-day matters that people have to think about, many do not take the time to think about matters of the heart. They take very little time for introspection to ponder on what resonates within them. This oversight, oftentimes unintentional, means that the essence of what could be their legacy often remains unexplored, tucked away in the recesses of their minds and daily routines.

## Legacy Matters Key #31

***Your thoughts reflect what is in your heart.***

Those who build a legacy greater than their wildest dreams are the ones who consciously choose to do so and are deliberate and intentional about their thoughts, actions and deeds. Creating your legacy requires contemplating what matters and asking yourself, "What do I want to leave with my family, community and the world, and how can I bring this desire into reality?"

Oftentimes, people shy away from thinking about their potential legacy because they have the misconception that legacy is solely about material wealth or resources. Nothing is further from the truth. Creating your legacy begins with something as straightforward as introspection. *"What do I have in my heart to do? How do I want to be remembered."*

Ultimately, I believe that deep inside, most people desire to positively impact the lives of their immediate family members, their spouses, significant others, children, grandchildren, great grandchildren and generations to follow. They are good people who wish to contribute meaningfully and make a difference. However, the challenge is in their perception. They often fail to recognize their potential to make a difference, as their personal struggles overshadow their ability to see the significance of their lives to others. Their "struggle" becomes their struggle, but the struggle starts in the heart. The true battle begins in the heart. Your thoughts reflect what is in your heart. Ultimately, the struggle is in the mind.

The question is, what is really in your heart? If you are unsure what is in your heart, you will be unable to adequately create your legacy. It starts with the desires of your heart because God gives you the desires of your heart.

**God Calls The Family**

God has a unique plan for every family. He calls every family to a particular purpose in life. The purpose and plan that He has given to the head of the family is not just for the matriarch and/or the patriarch to fulfill. It is an assignment that is supposed to be completed by the family together, not solo. I am referring to building something that lasts, something that more than just one person can accomplish, but something that outlasts you, your children, your grandchildren and beyond. We are called to collaborate as a family unit, a collective, working together as a team, building a legacy that is centered on us.

## Legacy Matters Key #32

***God calls every family to a particular purpose in life.***

Matthew 22:32 says, *"I am the God of Abraham, Isaac, and Jacob."* This denotes a family lineage, one marked by divine guidance. This passage of scripture highlights the importance of acknowledging God's presence across generations. Jacob diverged from this path when he embraced foreign gods, leading himself into trouble. It was during this tumultuous period that Jacob, much like Jesse, later realized the significance of returning to the faith of his forefathers. They acknowledged the God of their forefathers as the one true

God who rescued them, committing to worship Him as their ancestors did. That is legacy!

This return to faith exemplifies the concept of legacy, illustrating how, despite attempts to escape it, you cannot easily sever ties with your inherited destiny because it is embedded in your lineage, a purpose that the family is meant to fulfill. Jacob tried to diverge from the path of his forefathers, but he was unable to do it because legacy was in his bloodline. It was what the family was purposed to do.

The challenge often faced by younger generations stems from a lack of understanding of their parents' convictions and their family legacy. Without clear, intentional communication and demonstration of these values, children may find it hard to grasp and embrace this legacy. They see their parents engaging with their faith or traditions more out of habit than deliberate practice, making it difficult for them to fully comprehend or adopt these practices themselves. Understanding and living out one's legacy requires not just knowledge of family history or traditions but a deep connection to the intentions and beliefs of those who came before. It is difficult to do what you don't understand. *"Let this mind be in you that was also in Christ Jesus."* (Philippians 2:5)

# Legacy Matters Key #33

***The only way to leave an inheritance intentionally and deliberately for your children's children is to go within and give serious thought to your heart's desires.***

It should be our heart's desire to leave an inheritance for our children's children. Your legacy should run that deep and beyond. However, the only way to leave an inheritance intentionally and deliberately for your children's children is to go within and give serious thought to your heart's desires. The key is to think from the mind of God so that your heart's desires reflect the purpose and plan of God for your life.

In John 5:19, Jesus said, *"Verily, verily, I say unto you, The Son can do nothing of himself, but what he seeth the Father do: for what things soever he doeth, these also doeth the Son likewise."* In other words, Jesus said his only purpose in life was to do what the Father did. His focus was on leaving a legacy and on the act of creation.

Career paths tend to run in families. For instance, when a parent's career is a doctor or a lawyer, it is common for their children to pursue careers in the same fields. Often, if the family includes multiple children, at least one of the children will follow directly in their parent's footsteps, becoming a doctor or lawyer themselves. This trend suggests a blend of influence and inspiration, where children are drawn to professions that mirror their parents' careers. It highlights the impact of family role models on career choices. This is the impact of legacy and the significance of family connectedness in building a strong legacy.

One thing I have observed, much to my dismay, is that many children want to differentiate themselves from their parents and "pave their own way." They fight to not be like their parents. They resist following in their parents' footsteps and emulating what their parents did – continuing the legacy of the family business; going to the same university; working in the same profession. This often stems from a lack of awareness and understanding of the significance of legacy, which underscores the importance of teaching the value of legacy to our children, grandchildren, and communities.

In 2018, LeBron James, a prominent and successful basketball player and icon of the NBA, took on a major philanthropic venture and founded the I Promise School, a school for at-risk children, in his hometown of Akron, Ohio. The I Promise School serves children from first to eighth grade. In 2023, it was reported that the school's standardized testing scores ranked among the lowest proficiency scores in the state of Ohio. Although LeBron's intentions were honorable, I am sure he did not intend for low performance statistics to be a part of his legacy.

LeBron's story depicts the importance of clearly communicating your values and convictions while you are living. If the I Promise School is a part of the legacy that LeBron James was commissioned by God to build, then he has to make it very clear that failure is not a part of his legacy and that regardless of what it looks like presently, the I Promise School and its students will be a success. As the founder of the school, I am sure he is not happy about its current state, but he has to make it very clear that the school's current performance does not testify to who he is and why he founded the school.

Think about it… if something were to happen to him today, his school and the educational part of his legacy would currently be regarded as a failure.

This does not imply that the current situation is beyond repair. It highlights that his initiative is perceived as a failure at the moment. Instituting a major educational venture and financially supporting it is not enough to build a legacy. LeBron James (including his family, leadership team and community) has to vocalize his disapproval of the school's current educational ranking and take the public stance that failure is not an option for the present and future children of the I Promise School. He has to declare boldly and loudly, "NOT ON MY WATCH!" And he and his family and community stakeholders have to be just as passionate and vocal as Lebron is about his basketball career and legacy, because the family is called to build and carry his same legacy.

## Legacy Matters Key #34

***It does not matter if you are a billionaire or an everyday worker, building your legacy has to be deliberate, methodical and intentional.***

The school's performance shows that somebody did not know LeBron's heart on the matter of education. It appears that the essence of his intentions was not captured in this project. His team must not have fully grasped his passion for education. His story of overcoming challenges as an inner-city youth and his goals clearly suggests a mismatch between the outcome and his genuine desires. This example reiterates the importance of being intentional and methodical in building your legacy.

At the end of the day, I believe LeBron James aspires for his legacy to extend beyond his status as a sports legend, which is honorable and powerful. However, it does not matter if you are a billionaire or an everyday worker, building your legacy has to be deliberate, methodical and intentional, and your family and community must know your heart in the matter and be committed to preserving your legacy.

**Sacrifice**

Building a legacy that outlives you and benefits future generations is an admirable endeavor. It is a venture that requires determination, vision, and sacrifice. However, bringing the future we imagine into our present reality demands that we lay down immediate pleasures for the long-term gains of those who will follow the roads that we have paved. In other words, it requires sacrifice. Building a meaningful legacy often demands the ultimate sacrifice.

You have to be willing to forfeit many of your present comforts and desires in order to build a powerful and positive legacy that will last for generations to come.

***"Truly, truly, I say to you, whoever believes in me will also do the works that I do; and greater works than these will he do, because I am going to the Father."***

***(John 14:12)***

Every generation must make the sacrifice for the generations to follow. That is the ultimate sacrifice. Let's look at Jesus. Jesus made the ultimate sacrifice by sacrificing his life for the betterment and advancement of humanity. His work is complete. But now it is leveraged to the next generation to do greater works. The question is, what are you going to do as a result of the ultimate sacrifice that He made for the generations that would follow Him?

# Legacy Matters Key #35

***Every generation must make a sacrifice, but one generation has to make the ultimate sacrifice.***

**Allow me to share a bit more of my story…**

*My wife and I have taken on this mantle of sacrifice for the good of our children, grandchildren, great-grandchildren and generations beyond. I would say we have made the ultimate sacrifice. We are the pioneers in our family who have taken on the responsibility of building a meaningful, stable and financially sound legacy. Now, let me be very clear. Neither my wife nor I grew up with a silver spoon in our mouths. As a matter of fact, quite the contrary. We were not born into generational wealth, nor did our parents talk about legacy building or wealth generation. We started from very little means. Yet, we chose to sacrifice in our present (and still are) to build a legacy that will extend well beyond our children and grandchildren.*

*Our efforts have been successful thus far and we have been able to enjoy some of the fruit of our labor. We have even had the privilege to help not only our children, but our parents as well. But we still have to make the sacrifice. There are things that we can do that we choose not to do because we understand the power and purpose and the importance of legacy. We are building a legacy and leaving a blueprint for our children's children to continue and expand. We are intentionally leaving the how-to's and the why.*

There is always one generation that makes the ultimate sacrifice. Usually, that is the person who begins to recognize and communicate the importance of legacy.

***"Then Jesus told his disciples, 'If anyone would come after me, let him deny himself and take up his cross and follow me.'" (Matthew 16:24)***

Oftentimes, we have to deny ourselves so that other generations can benefit. There lies the challenge in legacy building. Who is the generation that is willing to make the ultimate sacrifice? Deny yourself so that you can generationally live - beyond one or two generations. Every generation must make a sacrifice, but one generation has to make the ultimate sacrifice.

## Legacy Matters Key #36

***The sacrifices you make intentionally build the legacy that will endure and bless your family for generations to come.***

Who is going to be that generation? Think about it - the reason some people do not leave a legacy is because they are selfish and self-centered. It does not matter if you are at the beginning of constructing your legacy or if you are rewriting your narrative (like my wife and I did), the truth is that legacy requires sacrifice. Let me underscore that. Leaving a legacy demands making sacrifices.

Someone must take the initiative and make the hard choices that will turn dreams into reality. Someone has to make that ultimate sacrifice for something bigger than themselves in order to leave behind a legacy that will span generations. The sacrifices you make - including the immediate luxuries that you choose to forego, the long hours that you work, and the close management of the resources that you have - intentionally build the legacy that will endure and bless your family for generations to come.

**Die Empty**

***"Whatever your hand finds to do, do it with your might, for there is no work or thought or knowledge or wisdom in Sheol, to which you are going.***

***(Ecclesiastes 9:10)***

God deposited within all of us everything we need to be successful, everything we need to fulfill our destiny and purpose, everything that we need to fulfill that which He created us to be. We expand, grow and develop as we become more and more aware of our purpose here on earth. It is our responsibility to do the work. Once we have become aware of who God has created us to be, we have to then do the work of multiplying what God placed in our hands, so much so that we fill the earth. That is legacy.

***"And God blessed them and said to them, Be fruitful, multiply, and fill the earth, and subdue it [using all its vast resources in the service of God and man]; and have dominion over the fish of the sea, the birds of the air, and over every living creature that moves upon the earth." (Genesis 1:28, Amplified Version)***

To "fill the earth," means we are to release what God has invested in us back into the earth where we complete everything that He has purposed for us, which is our created purpose. It means to be able to die in peace and at peace, knowing that you were able to empty your life of what God invested in you. As a result of emptying your life, you will be able to see what I call the perpetual harvest, the harvest that lasts indefinitely. The deposit that God made in us is considered to be a seed, and as such, we have been given the responsibility by God to release that seed back into the ground. We have to die empty.

# Legacy Matters Key #37

***Your created purpose, acts as both your compass and your guide, steering you through life's decisions.***

Dying empty means to die having lived a full, purposeful, meaningful life. It is a process that begins as soon as you become aware of what you were commissioned by God to do from birth. First, you have to recognize, acknowledge and embrace who God created you to be. Second, you have to mold, shape and hone the gifts that God has given to you in order to creatively live out what you have been purposed to do from the beginning. Once you acknowledge and recognize your created purpose, you have to develop, grow and shape those things that God has placed within you and begin to make intentional and deliberate decisions in life that align with that created purpose.

Your created purpose acts as both your compass and your guide, steering you through life's decisions. It is those things that clearly align with your life's purpose. You should navigate your course in life, your decisions and choices, based on your created purpose. This creative direction will help you shape a meaningful life purpose. Proverbs 10:4 says, *"He becomes poor who works with a slack and idle hand, but the hand of the diligent makes rich."* Once you discover who you are and your purpose in life, you then have the responsibility to put forth the effort to ensure that everything you put your hands to do will be done with diligence to ensure that your purpose is lived out.

***"For I am now ready to be offered, and the time of my departure is at hand. I have fought a good fight, I have finished my course, I have kept the faith: Henceforth there is laid up for me a crown of righteousness, which the Lord, the righteous judge, shall give me at that day: and not to me only, but unto all them also that love his appearing." (2 Timothy 4:6-8)***

In 2 Timothy 4:6-8, Paul exemplifies the concept of legacy and the power of dying empty. Essentially, Paul stayed committed to his divine assignment and fulfilled what he was created to do. Not only did he stay the course, but he completed his journey. Paul was nearing the end of his life when he penned these words, yet he retained all his mental faculties. He was fully cognizant and capable of expressing that he had nothing left undone. He had accomplished everything he was meant to accomplish. Despite every obstacle, battle, and hardship, he was still able to finish everything and die empty. Not only did he finish, but he finished well and remained faithful.

# Legacy Matters Key #38

***Legacy is part of filling the earth with what God has purposed, called, ordained, and created you to be and to become.***

In the course of our lives, we are going to be involved in a number of conflicts that will put our faith to the test and test the foundation of our beliefs. At the end of our lives, each of us should have the opportunity to reflect on our life's journey and be able to make a declaration similar to Paul's. Paul's message is about facing death without fear, knowing that he emptied out, completed his assignment, ran his race to the end and did what he was supposed to do. What a powerful way to die. Not only that, but he also passed the baton to Timothy, showcasing an element of thoughtful succession planning. Paul's life highlights the importance of leaving behind a foundation upon which the next generation can build.

***"Thus says the Lord, your Redeemer, the Holy One of Israel: I am the Lord your God, Who teaches you to profit, Who leads you in the way that you should go." (Isaiah 48:17)***

God teaches us to profit, prosper, reproduce, and fill the earth. How am I going to fill the earth? I am going to fill the earth with His glory by living out what He has purposed me to do. Filling the earth has nothing to do with material possessions. Filling the earth means dying empty. It means filling the earth with your purpose, your assignment, your calling.

# Legacy Matters Key #39

***Everything we see in the natural dies and goes back to its origin. But the one thing that does not die is the spirit.***

We have a responsibility to fill the earth. God never created anything that is not self-sufficient. The earth has been created to sustain itself. So, when God says to fill the earth, he is not talking about more earth. There is nothing else that the earth needs other than what God has purposed and created you to do to fill it. Legacy is part of filling the earth with what God has purposed, called, ordained, and created you to be and to become. God is referring to the spirit of the thing. Fill the earth with the spirit of what I created you to be, because the spirit lives forever. That in and of itself is amazing.

God is instructing us to do what He did. Watch what God does in the book of Genesis. Genesis 1:27 reads, *"So God created man in his own image, in the image of God created he him; male and female created he them."* He creates man and places man in the Earth. But man does not have the ability to do what God purposed man to do until He blows into man. *"And the LORD God formed man of the dust of the ground, and breathed into his nostrils the breath of life; and man became a living soul."* (Genesis 2:7) Man does not become a living being until God blows into man and man becomes, the Bible says, a living speaking God.

The breath of God endowed Man with the same power to govern and create. Now, for his potential to be realized Man must blow into the earth. Our life is the source of the breath that fills the earth. The breath that fills the earth comes from the life you live. The legacy left behind imbues the world with God's spirit. Without the breath that God breathed into Man, he is nothing more than dust.

So, when God blew into man, man became a living, speaking God. Essentially, God said, *"I have put my nature in you to be able to operate in the earth as me. Now, it is your turn to fill the earth. Blow into it your intent with the creative nature that I that I blew into you. Fill the earth with your presence, your spirit, your DNA by fulfilling the purpose and the assignment that I have assigned, blessed and ordained for you."*

**What's In The Dust?**

***"And the LORD God formed man of the dust of the ground, and breathed into his nostrils the breath of life; and man became a living soul." (Genesis 2:7)***

In Genesis 2:7, God formed man out of the dust of the ground and breathed into man the breath of life. Dust is not just a collection of tiny particles on the ground. Man was made from the dust of the ground. The very essence of God is found in the dust. The awareness of God and the consciousness of God are buried deep within the dust. The spirit of man is in the dust.

# Legacy Matters Key #40

***You are a spirit being having a human experience here on earth.***

The dust serves as the dwelling place for the spirit of man to live. So, what is in the dust? The nature of God is in the dust. The nature of God refers to the features that define him as God and divine. God is not concerned with dust as much as he is what is in the dust. The dust houses the spirit man, which is greater.

The nature of God is comprised of his attributes and his characteristics. That is what makes him God. It speaks to the divinity of God.

1) **GOD IS OMNISCIENT** - all knowing. *"Howbeit when he, the Spirit of truth, is come, he will guide you into all truth: for he shall not speak of himself; but whatsoever he shall hear, that shall he speak: and he will shew you things to come"* (John 16:13). The Holy Spirit will guide you into all truth. There is no truth that exists that I do not have access to if I yield myself to the power of the Holy Spirit. That is omniscience.

2) **GOD IS OMNIPRESENT** – everywhere at the same time. The Holy Spirit lives within us. Have you ever been in a space where you can sense a person's presence? They are not physically in the space, but you can feel their presence. That is omnipresence.

3) **GOD IS OMNIPOTENT** – all powerful. Deuteronomy 8:18 says, *"But thou shalt remember the LORD thy God: for it is he that giveth thee power to get wealth..."* God has given us the power to operate in the earth like Him. He has given us creative power, healing power, and the power to get wealth. That is omnipotence.

Together these attributes comprise the nature of God. It is what makes Him God. The very same attributes of God described above are found in the dust (within you). You embody the nature of God. You have the power within you to create whatever you desire. You have the power to amass wealth. That is the power of legacy.

# Legacy Matters Key #41

***Your goal should be to craft a legacy that speaks volumes, not just about your goodness, but your greatness.***

So, legacy matters. Your goal should be to create a legacy that speaks volumes, not just about our goodness, but your greatness. In doing so, we never die. Our legacy lives for generations because of the significant deposit we leave in the earth. The spirit of your greatness must continue to live for generations. How do you do this? By building a powerful legacy while you are living. When you start is not as important as how you start.

**Allow me to share a bit more of my story...**

*I personally want to leave a deposit in the earth that lives beyond the life that I lived on earth. I want to leave behind something that goes on record to say not only that I was a good man, but I was a great man, one who cared about others more than he did himself. I want to be remembered as somebody that mattered. Why? Because people matter.*

*I want my children and my grandchildren to focus not only on the material things that I leave behind, but on the philanthropic endeavors that I led and the significant impact that we made in our family, community and the world. I want them to be able to look back with pride and say, "My dad meant a lot to me. My dad was something special. My grandfather was extraordinary. He made a difference in the lives of many, transforming not just a community but the world. The world is a better place because he lived."*

Everyone is creating a legacy, whether you know it or not. Whether you are creating your legacy intentionally or unintentionally, you are creating a legacy. The question is are you creating the legacy that you desire or is your legacy being created by default? That is something to really ponder. You have to be very clear and confident that the world is a better place because you lived. Legacy never dies.

# Legacy Matters Key #42

***Legacy never dies.***

When you do the work that we are talking about, you never die. The power of legacy is it never dies. If you create a legacy that impacts your loved ones and community after you leave the earth, you will never die. If you go ahead and build your legacy intentionally, you never die because something is in place that will always keep you here.

People with real wealth live intentionally and they make sure their legacy lives long after they leave the earth. A great example is St. Jude Children's Research Hospital. Danny Thomas, founder of St. Jude said, *"A dream is one thing. A realization is something entirely separate."* His philanthropic efforts have outlived him. His life and work still speaks volumes in the world today. Creating a lasting, impactful and life-rich legacy allows you to see death from a different perspective. Create an impactful legacy and you will never die. You will always live, because your work will outlive you. Legacy is not just about being remembered, but about influencing generations far into the future.

# CHAPTER FIVE:
# KINGDOM MATTERS

***"Declaring the end and the result from the beginning, and from ancient times the things that are not yet done, saying, My counsel shall stand, and I will do all My pleasure and purpose." (Isaiah 46:10)***

**The Balcony of Heaven**

There is one key component to this legacy building journey that is a game-changer – the kingdom matters when it comes to legacy. The revelation and understanding of the kingdom of God that lives within you will cause you to see your life through a different set of lenses.

Many people go through life thinking that the only time to connect with God is on Sundays, or Saturdays, or whenever their Sabbath is to worship, limiting their experience to those brief moments without really encountering the fullness of God. They fail to see the creative nature of God and how His word and creativity are being put into practice in their everyday lives.

## Legacy Matters Key #43

***The kingdom of God is within you.***

Relegating God to the "Sunday morning experience" limits the power of God from working fully in your life. You run the risk of overlooking the countless ways in which God's creativity can be experienced in your own personal life. It also limits you from fully recognizing and embracing the presence of God in you, in the world, in your relationships, and in the challenges and triumphs of daily life. The manifestation of God's word is more than just hearing or reading it; it encompasses the tangible expression of God's presence through our actions, choices, and interactions with the world around us. When it comes to legacy, the kingdom matters!

I have been in church all of my life, from my childhood through adulthood, but I have observed how "going to church" can become a vicious cycle. As a child, my family took me to church every Sunday, yet I never saw real transformation in our personal lives. We repeated the same cycle Sunday after Sunday, but our lives remained the same, always struggling, living from paycheck to paycheck, never really experiencing the prosperity, the power and the presence of God as depicted in God's word. As I got older, I realized that God's presence in my life had to extend beyond the confines of Sunday worship, Bible study, and Vacation Bible School.

As an apostle, pastor, prophet, and mentor, I believe that the revelation of the kingdom of God within us must be taught to people so that they understand the power that is inside of them. Jesus said in Luke 17:21, *"...for, behold, the kingdom of God is within you."* The kingdom of God lives in you whether you are aware of it or not. The "kingdom message" and understanding that the kingdom lives inside of me, caused me to manifest my heart's desires and experience heaven on earth. This revelation changed everything about me and how I navigated my life. It caused me to live life at a greater level and to dream bigger. It revolutionized my entire being and approach to life. Everything in my life changed when I became aware that the kingdom of God lives within me.

## Legacy Matters Key #44

***You can only be what you see.***

Many people believe that the culmination of their lives occurs at death. I often hear believers say, *"When I get to heaven what a time I will have."* Hebrews 12, talks about the great cloud of witnesses that we have in heaven.

***"Wherefore seeing we also are compassed about with so great a cloud of witnesses, let us lay aside every weight, and the sin which doth so easily beset us, and let us run with patience the race that is set before us" (Hebrews 12:1)***

This great cloud of witnesses laid the foundations of faith for us. Now, from beyond they watch not only to see how their work turns out, but also to cheer us on as we go through life, achieve our goals, and fulfill the divine purpose within us. They are our fan base encouraging us to greatness, cheering us on as we pursue life, our purpose, and the things God placed inside of us.

You should not wait until you get to heaven and can see from heaven's balcony, to understand and appreciate the importance of what you are doing now to build your legacy. Instead, make it a priority to appreciate and rejoice in what you have accomplished while on earth and celebrate the fruit of your labor, and be encouraged that there is a great cloud of witnesses with you cheering you on from the balcony of heaven.

We are spirit beings, have an earthly experience. Therefore, we have the ability to see from another dimension what God has planned, purposed and prepared for our lives. By learning to look beyond your current circumstances and view your life through the eyes of your spirit man, you can see from the balcony of heaven the reality you desire to manifest in the earth. You can only be what you see. This is a key principle in building a lasting legacy that encompasses your desires and biggest hopes and dreams. You possess the capacity to perceive from a different dimension what God has envisioned, intended, and arranged for your life.

## Legacy Matters Key #45

***Heaven is now because heaven is right here on earth.***

You do not have to wait to get to heaven to look over the balcony of heaven. That is called living life in reverse. Like God, you too can know the end from the beginning (Isaiah 46:10). What do you desire? What is your dream? What legacy do you want to create?

**Take a moment and begin to imagine…**

***Imagine this balcony of heaven, a place of beauty lifted high at a vantage point from where you can look over and see what God has for you. It is not just a physical structure; it is a spiritual place where there are no boundaries or limitations. It's a place of peace. Feel the glow as you look at what God has given you to create, manage, orchestrate and fill the earth. It is from this vantage point you begin to imagine the rich legacy that you are to intentionally create and leave for your family and community to enjoy for generations to come.***

**Heaven on Earth**

Heaven is akin to living your best life - a life of opulence and excellence, a life that is full and fulfilling. Heaven is the word of God being manifested in the flesh in our world. It presents itself as a life marked by prosperity, abundance and a meaningful legacy. It is living life to its maximum potential in alignment with what God promised in His Word, without limitations.

Experiencing heaven on earth means possessing a storehouse of good that is available to those who know how to access what God has provided. In heaven (the mind of God) there are no boundaries or restrictions. Heaven has whatever you need. It is just a matter of accessing these blessings and divine provisions of God by faith. Heaven signifies a place of peace. Imagine a haven of peace, abundance, and provision, a place where healing manifests, ensuring wholeness in mind, body, and spirit. That, my friend, is heaven on earth.

## Legacy Matters Key #46

***There are no limits to what you can imagine and create.***

There are no limits in God, no boundaries, no limitations. That is the power of legacy. Many people think they have to have a business, or property, or a large sum of money to leave a legacy. That is a fallacy. You are not limited to the city or state where you live. The earth is your real estate property. Dream and create as big as you desire. There are no limits.

I am sure you have heard the saying, "The sky is the limit." But even that imposes a limit – the sky. There are absolutely no limits in God. There are no limits to what you can achieve or how successful you can be. The possibilities are endless. There are no constraints on your potential to reach your dreams and goals. The possibilities are boundless and limitless.

The more you understand the attributes of God presented earlier in this book – His omniscience, His omnipresence and His omnipotence – and realize that these same attributes are within you, the more confidence you will have in creating your legacy. The greater your awareness of the kingdom of God within you, the more power you will have. Why? Because you are an heir of God and a joint heir with Jesus Christ.

***"And if children, then heirs; heirs of God, and joint-heirs with Christ; if so be that we suffer with him, that we may be also be glorified together. For I reckon that the sufferings of this present time are not worthy to be compared with the glory which shall be revealed in us. For the earnest expectation of the creature waiteth for the manifestation of the sons of God." (Romans 8:17-19)***

An heir is one who inherits the spiritual and material goods that have been left by a family member who has gone before him. An heir is usually legally entitled because he is in the family. You are a child of God, which makes you an heir of God, and a joint heir with Jesus Christ. What a clear picture of legacy. Legacy really does matter. When we accept and acknowledge God as our Source, we are engrafted into the family of God, thereby becoming heirs to the promises of God. We become partakers of his divine nature. *"Whereby are given unto us exceeding great and precious promises: that by these ye might be partakers of the divine nature..."* (2 Peter 1:4)

## Legacy Matters Key #47

***The efforts and the sacrifices we make, along with the processes that we go through to create our legacy require deliberate and intentional action.***

Romans 8:18 says, *"For I reckon that the sufferings of this present time are not worthy to be compared with the glory which shall be revealed in us."* This scripture is not just speaking of when we leave this life and go to heaven. It depicts heaven on earth. The efforts and the sacrifices we make, along with the processes that we go through to create our legacy require deliberate and intentional action. As I shared in the previous chapter, legacy requires sacrifice. Each generation must sacrifice for the benefit of the generations to follow. When God observes a man or woman who embodies legacy, it not only brings glory to His name, but it also brings glory to heaven itself. Heaven receives glory when God sees a person who is living life intentionally, guided by the principles of legacy.

Romans 8:19 continues, *"For the earnest expectation of the creature waiteth for the manifestation of the sons of God."* A true son embraces his inheritance and lives out his heirship. Creation is waiting for us to take our rightful position on earth. What is this position? Your rightful position is an heir of the kingdom of God. You demonstrate the power of legacy when you walk in your heirship because you not only show that you are a son/daughter of the living God, but you are embracing your inheritance as an heir.

We want our children to grow up, achieve their highest potential, and have everything they need. Similarly, God desires the same for us. Living a life of abundance reflects where you come from. You represent the manifestation of your family's legacy. However, achieving this does not come without its challenges, including struggle, sacrifice, and suffering. The biggest obstacles people face in living out the legacy intended for them by God are the struggle, sacrifice and suffering that comes with it. That is why only a small fraction of people, the so-called "one percenters," manage to realize such a legacy. They are willing to go through the struggle, the sacrifice, and the suffering in order to change their family legacy to manifest their divine heirship. Do you think that Bill Gates' children are concerned about anything that money can buy? Absolutely not.

## Legacy Matters Key #48

***The power of awareness is the power to change.***

As an heir to the kingdom of God, you have the responsibility of accessing and sharing the blessings of heaven that are available not only to you but also to those entrusted to your care. It is about making sure that your family, loved ones and community, be it in life or in death, gets what they deserve. Think about it: everything you do, every move you make, it's all part of the story you are leaving behind. Every action you take in life is linked to the legacy you leave behind.

The more aware you are of who God created you to be, the more you are able to change and control the story of your life at any moment. The power of awareness is the power to change. My goal is to raise your level of awareness of who God created you to be and the God-nature within you to build a powerful, meaningful, and impactful legacy that will bless your family and community for generations to come. This God-nature within you to "fill the earth" gives you the ability to overcome any challenges that may appear to stand in the way of you being and becoming everything God has destined for you from the beginning.

Regardless of your current circumstances, recognizing and embracing this God-nature triggers an internal realization that you are equipped with everything necessary to accomplish your God-given purpose. This revelation is pivotal, as it strengthens your determination to fulfill the assignment that God has called you to do in the earth.

Kingdom matters. Understanding this concept is a key component in building your legacy, as it goes beyond the mechanical actions of building your legacy or the possessions you accumulate. It requires you to have a higher level of consciousness and confidence that you can create a strong legacy that will bless and empower your family. It requires a shift towards a higher state of awareness and self-assuredness. You must be aware of the possibilities of leaving a legacy that will last for generations to come or the opportunity to create one from scratch. Anybody serious about knowing their purpose, as well as the lasting impact they are capable of creating, must make this mental shift.

# Legacy Matters Key #49

***The spirit of God within you and the revelation of the kingdom is the secret to building a lasting, impactful legacy.***

At this moment, some of you reading this book will say, "Wow… all of that is in me?" Yes! It is within you. The kingdom of God is within you! God wants you to think generationally. That is why He breathed so much into you. Start walking in that power. Generations matters to God, and it should matter to you. I want you to develop such a deep revelation of legacy that it moves you to manifestation and ultimately, glorification. Glorification is where we bring glory to God by filling the earth with what He placed inside of us. The spirit of God within you and the revelation of the kingdom is the secret to building a lasting, impactful legacy. At the end of our life's journey, the body (this earth suit) goes back to the ground (buried or cremated). But if you consciously, intentionally, and deliberately fill the earth with the essence of who God is in you, your spirit will never die.

**The Advantage**

***"For we wrestle not against flesh and blood, but against principalities, against powers, against the rulers of the darkness of this world, against spiritual wickedness in high places." (Ephesians 6:12)***

Your life's purpose takes on a new meaning when you realize that you have been born into God's kingdom. You have the advantage. In my journey of building legacy, I have faced significant challenges in my faith, battling not just tangible issues but also spiritual ones. I've been in some great faith fights with the system. But Ephesians 6:12 teaches us that our struggles are not physical, but our struggles are against spiritual forces. This realization is game-changing. The moment you identify the principality, you have the ability to overcome.

When you shift your view of the battle from a physical to a spiritual one, acknowledging that you are not fighting against people but against spiritual entities, you position yourself for victory. You set yourself up for success when you change the focus of the conflict, realizing that we are not battling against humans but against forces of the spirit realm. Many people focus on the physical aspect, attempting to fight tangible battles. But once you identify the spiritual forces challenging your legacy, your family, your finances and your life, you unlock the potential to overcome these adversities.

## Legacy Matters Key #50

***Once you identify the principality that is coming against your legacy, you set yourself up to win.***

You cannot win a spiritual fight if you fight from the flesh. Once you identify the principality that is coming against your legacy, you set yourself up to win. God has given us authority over principalities.

**Allow me to share a bit more of my story…**

*I encountered a major fight while spearheading a project that seemed unthinkable for a Black man to undertake, especially in the area in which I live. This experience was one of the most significant tests of faith that I have ever encountered. I was confronted with an unprecedented level of racism and animosity directed at me solely because of my faith. I found myself struggling primarily because I approached the conflict on a personal level, constantly reminding myself of my identity as a Black man and perceiving the resistance as a refusal by others to see me succeed.*

*As long as I viewed the situation through this lens, the systemic barriers prevailed. Everything changed when I felt God challenge me to shift my focus. I felt the omniscience of God well up within me and I realized that I had to identify the principality. I had to look beyond the surface to recognize the underlying forces at play. It was in that moment that I realized that racism is a principality. It is a spirit. Racism is more than just individual prejudice or a personal vendetta. It is a pervasive force, something that must be confronted on a spiritual level. I began to confront the principality, not the individual who was opposing me in the natural. I took the fight to the spirit realm where I was able to win.*

*Racism is real, but racism is a spirit. As a Black man, I experience racism from other races, as well as within my own race. Racism is a result of not understanding another culture. I periodically encounter a pervasive stereotype held by some within the Black community that suggests that Black people who are successful and have amassed substantial wealth are engaged in illegal activities if they are not athletes or celebrities.*

*I am a pastor, as well as an entrepreneur and wealth strategist. My role as a pastor introduces another dimension of scrutiny. People expect pastors to live modestly. Criticism arises from those within the Black community and from other racial groups, especially from those who hold traditional views about how clergy should live. Their view is that a pastor displaying wealth could be seen as prioritizing materialism over spirituality. Historically, it was also frowned upon for pastors to be bi-vocational, adding another layer of complexity to how my lifestyle is perceived.*

*Each of these factors contributes to the scrutiny of my lifestyle choices, highlighting the challenges of navigating personal success and public perception as both a Black man and a pastor. But the kingdom of God and the revelation I have of the kingdom of God within me gives me the advantage. There are no limitations to the success I can achieve. My goal is to create as many opportunities for wealth generation as I can so that I can be a blessing to my family and my community and leave a legacy that speaks long after I have transitioned from this life.*

If you believe in the power of God and the power of the kingdom, then you have the power to overcome any obstacle that will attempt to keep you from being and becoming who God has ordained. The kingdom of God gives you the advantage.

***"Jesus answered him, I assure you, most solemnly I tell you, that unless a person is born again (anew, from above), he cannot ever see (know, be acquainted with, and experience) the kingdom of God." (John 3:3, Amplified Version)***

The kingdom of God system is a government. It is the power and authority that we have been given as believers to operate by a set of principles and precepts that give us the advantage in life. It is a government that has power and authority over any other system. The kingdom of God is not of this world. It is a spirit world that exists outside of this world. The kingdom of God is a system that supersedes any other system. The extent to which we understand the kingdom is directly proportional to the degree to which we can function inside the kingdom and experience the power of the kingdom of God.

## Legacy Matters Key #51

***The extent to which we understand the kingdom is directly proportional to the degree to which we can function inside the kingdom and experience the power of the kingdom of God.***

***"Neither shall they say, Lo here! or, lo there! for, behold, the kingdom of God is within you." (Luke 17:21)***

The kingdom of God is within you. Many people are trying to get what they already have. You already possess the keys that are necessary to create the life that you desire. The challenge with most believers is they have no revelation that the kingdom exists. Allow me to let you in on a secret. Just because you have no revelation that the kingdom of God is within you, does not mean that it doesn't exist. Luke 17:21 is emphasizing that you possess everything you need to create the life and the legacy that you desire, because the kingdom of God is within you.

God has already placed within you everything you need to be successful and create the legacy that will bless your children, grandchildren and generations to come. However, human beings can only do what they know. Just because someone is not aware of the kingdom of God within them, does not mean it's not real. Just because you are not aware that God has no limits, does not mean that limits exist. Brace yourself for this next truth… Every limitation you experience is self-imposed. The truth is there are unlimited resources in the kingdom of God.

# Legacy Matters Key #52

***Every limitation you experience is self-imposed.***

The Bible says in 1 John 4:4, "...*Greater is he that is in you, than he that is in the world.*" Do you hold this to be true for your life? If so, then nothing can stand in the way of you establishing and shaping your legacy, whether it be through amassing wealth or whatever you consider to be your legacy's components. The only person who can stop you is you.

**Revelation of Need**

***"But my God shall supply all your need according to his riches in glory by Christ Jesus." (Philippians 4:19)***

Philippians 4:19 says that God will supply all your need according to his riches in glory. You cannot claim that God will meet your need and then limit Him. Supply is relegated to what you *believe* you need. So, what is need? Need is relative to the person you ask. We have basic needs for food, water, shelter, clothing. How that need is met is relative to what you deem is your need. Your need is based on your revelation of what you <u>can</u> need.

For example, if my need is a three-bedroom/two-bathroom house based on what I believe I can have or what I can afford or what has been afforded to me by the government, then I will only seek God for a three-bedroom/two-bathroom house. If my need is to make enough money to pay my bills each month and I do not give any thought to having extra money (since I only need to get by), then my supply is relegated to what I deem as my need. God cannot go beyond what I believe Him for. It goes back to self-imposed limitations.

Your need may be a Hyundai or a Honda. Someone else's need may be a Rolls Royce or a Bentley. The same God supplies our need, but He meets us each at the point of our need. The difference between the Hyundai and the Honda and the Bentley and the Rolls Royce is your revelation of your need. We limit God based on our revelation of need.

For one person their need may be Versace, because for their level of consciousness Versace is comfortable. However, for someone else, their desire may be something more modest, and still others may contend that Versace isn't necessary. The definition of a "need" varies substantially among people. What is considered a need can vary greatly from person to person. While some may claim they do not need a million dollars, this does not hold true for everyone. My need is at the multimillion dollar level. Why? I understand the assignment on my life. I am aware of my God-ordained purpose.

Your need is usually based on your environment and your upbringing. Some people have a need to supersede their parents' accomplishments. If your need is to just purchase a house, that is the extent that God will provide. Once I got a revelation there is nowhere in the Bible God says He will give you "a house" but the Bible says He will give you "houses," my wife and I took God at His word and began to amass wealth through real estate, because we realized the earth is our real estate property. When you are definitive about the legacy that you want to live on in your family and community and you recognize what you will need to manifest it, God will supply your need. God has already equipped you with abundant resources to fulfill that desire.

## Legacy Matters Key #53

***Need is intrinsically related to your purpose in life.***

Need has everything to do with assignment. It is assignment driven. Our assignment motivates our need. Everyone does not have a need for a jet. Perhaps their assignment does not call for a jet. Our individual assignments will decide what we need in the end. As soon as you understand your God-given assignment, you will realize the need and the supply that is associated with that assignment.

***"Now unto him that is able to do exceeding abundantly above all that we ask or think, according to the power that worketh in us." (Ephesians 3:20)***

Ephesians 3:20 says that God will do exceeding abundantly, and far above all you can ask, think or imagine. If you can imagine it, then you are thinking too small. It is far from what God desires to do in your life. What legacy do you desire to leave for your family? Are you thinking too small? Are you dreaming big? Only you can answer these questions.

Think about it. If you have the kingdom consciousness and the power of God is within you, yet you are not currently building a legacy that empowers your children's children, then you are living below your means. Remember, Proverbs 13:22 says, *"A good man leaves an inheritance for his children's children."* If we are heirs of God and joint heirs with Jesus Christ, then how is it possible for God not to grant us the ability to build the kind of wealth that will have an impact on future generations?

## Legacy Matters Key #54

***God is not broke!***

God is not broke. He gives us the power to amass wealth (Deuteronomy 8:18). For some people, their minds are too small to conceive what God really desires to do in their lives. The moment I got that revelation and began to comprehend that my requests, thoughts, and dreams were too small, then I realized that there was nothing too big for me to believe God to manifest in my life. This insight necessitates a continuous renewal of the mind. No matter how far you've come in this journey, you must continuously renew your mind, because everything around you may say something different.

# CHAPTER SIX:
# COMMUNITY MATTERS

***"Thou shalt love thy neighbour as thyself." (Matthew 22:39)***

**People Matter**

People matter because God said we matter. There is an innate aspect of each of us, inherently designed by God that makes us relational and draws us to connect with each other. Our relational nature is an essential component of who we are. It compels us to engage and interact with people around us. People play a significant part in our lives and in the larger framework of what actually matters. We naturally want to connect with other people. Relationships, interpersonal bonds, and human connection are important for giving life purpose and meaning. While each person has their own groups that are significant to them, everyone is valuable. What matters is how we engage with one another in community.

## Legacy Matters Key #55

***It is important to plan and document how you want your story to end.***

If you were to die today, what would your community say about you? Think about some of our legendary musical artists and actors who have died. Their philanthropic efforts often go unnoticed, overshadowed by their talents, achievements and the wealth they accumulated. Some managed to maintain their wealth, while others experienced losses for various reasons, including inadequate legal preparation and the absence of proper legal documents when they died. Even at such stature in life, these aspects of their lives frequently remain incomplete and unspoken.

If someone were to ask me what stands out about the former president of the United States, President Barak Obama, I would first highlight that he was the first Black president of the United States. This is not to overlook his other accomplishments. It is an observation that his contributions and achievements might not be fully acknowledged within our community or globally. For many, his signature achievement is the Affordable Care Act, also known as Obamacare, which was a significant milestone. Whether or not we agree with what his legacy is and will be, we must agree that he has made a significant impact in our world.

Beyond your immediate family and distant relatives, how will people remember the impact you made on their lives? This highlights the importance of being deliberate about the legacy you desire to create and leave for your family and community. It is important to plan and document how you want your story to end. Otherwise, you risk leaving your narrative to be interpreted by others based on their perception of your life, achievements and purpose, rather than your own.

What is going to be the gift that keeps on giving after the celebrations of your life are over. These interpretations will inevitably be shaped by what we value most. We should all contemplate what legacy we want to leave behind - the gift that continues to impact others long after the celebrations have ceased. Identifying this legacy and ensuring its longevity is essential beyond the work.

## Legacy Matters Key #56

***Legacy is not about the shine.***

This is the work to which my wife and I are committed. We have established several 501(c)(3) organizations in recent years as part of this effort. These entities are instrumental in how we have managed to make a positive difference in our communities through the outreach programs of our church and beyond. The importance of community is at the heart of our endeavors.

There was a church in Alabama that our church acquired some years back. The fate of this church was transformed as a result of a member who lived nearby. His modest way of life contradicts his actual wealth. Upon his passing, he bequeathed $800,000 to the church, a gesture that changed the life of the church. His generous donation enabled the church to relocate and embark on a new chapter. For some people, ensuring the church's financial stability is their legacy.

Many people engage in philanthropy quietly, seeking no recognition. Legacy transcends accolades. Legacy is not about the shine. It is about the spirit and impact of one's contributions. It is about what you leave in the earth that will be remembered long after you are gone.

It takes a community to build a legacy. People matter. Reflecting on Joshua 4:21, when the children of Israel crossed the Jordan, they were instructed to place twelve stones so their children would see them and ask, *"What do these stones mean?"*

***15 And the LORD spake unto Joshua, saying, 16 Command the priests that bear the ark of the testimony, that they come up out of Jordan. 17 Joshua therefore commanded the priests, saying, Come ye up out of Jordan. 18 And it came to pass, when the priests that bare the ark of the covenant of the LORD were come up out of the midst of Jordan, and the soles of the priests' feet were lifted up unto the dry land, that the waters of Jordan returned unto their place, and flowed over all his banks, as they did before. 19 And the people came up out of Jordan on the tenth day of the first month, and encamped in Gilgal, in the east border of Jericho.***

***20 And those twelve stones, which they took out of Jordan, did Joshua pitch in Gilgal. 21 And he spake unto the children of Israel, saying, When your children shall ask their fathers in time to come, saying, What mean these stones? 22 Then ye shall let your children know, saying, Israel came over this Jordan on dry land. 23 For the LORD your God dried up the waters of Jordan from before you, until ye were passed over, as the LORD your God did to the Red sea, which he dried up from before us, until we were gone over: 24 That all the people of the earth might know the hand of the LORD, that it is mighty: that ye might fear the LORD your God for ever. (Joshua 4:15-24)***

I found it interesting that God instructed the Israelites to pick up twelve stones - not ten, not seven. The number twelve symbolizes completion, perfection, divine authority, and government. In this passage, God instructs the Israelites as they cross the Jordan River. When God rolls back the waters, He commands them to take twelve stones from the riverbed. These stones are meant to signify the miracle of the waters parting, allowing them to walk through on dry land. The stones serve as a lasting reminder of how they overcame this challenge.

Similarly, in our lives, we must lay our own stones so that future generations might ask the same question. God wanted the children of Israel to never forget what He had done and all they had to go through to get to that place in their journey.

As I reflect on my life and legacy, it is very clear that if it had not been for the hand of the Lord on my life, along with the support of a community of partners and people who cared, there is no way I could have accomplished the things that God has allowed my family and I to accomplish. The stones serve not just as a reminder for our children but also for us to look back and be grateful to God and the people who have partnered with us in creating the life and legacy we now know.

I am deeply grateful to the Living Truth Church family and to the countless individuals who have made significant contributions to my life in ways I cannot fully express. Having pastored the Living Truth Church family for over 30 years, I recognize Living Truth as one of the significant stones in my life, one that holds immense importance and significance.

Community is the key difference maker in all our lives. I urge you to identify your twelve stones, which will represent the foundation of your legacy - perfection, completion, and divine authority. These stones will become the bedrock for your family, reflecting the core values and principles that define your legacy.

Have you identified those individuals who represent those significant stones in your life? Have you laid those stones so that when others look back and ask, "What do these stones mean," you will be able to say like me, "These stones symbolize the people, partners, and the love and guidance of God in my life." The songwriter penned the words, *"How I got over, my soul looks back and wonders how I got over."* For me, these stones are a representation of how I got over. We cannot do it without community.

**Your Unique Footprint**

***"And God blessed them, and God said unto them, Be fruitful, and multiply, and replenish the earth, and subdue it: and have dominion over the fish of the sea, and over the fowl of the air, and over every living thing that moveth upon the earth." (Genesis 1:28)***

God never gives us an instruction that He has not already put within us the ability to fulfill. Genesis 1:26-30 is God's blueprint for making every person on earth an entrepreneur/CEO to fulfill the mandate of legacy. The scripture says God "blessed them," meaning he empowered them to be fruitful.

God empowered them to be fruitful so that they could fulfill their legacy assignment, which was to leave an inheritance for their children's children. When God speaks, He speaks generationally.

## Legacy Matters Key #57

***God has given us the ability to affect generations by giving us dominion.***

The power of dominion is legacy. God placed within Adam and Eve the potential and ability to take dominion over the earth. In the same way, God has given us the ability to affect generations by giving us dominion. He gave us the power to amass wealth to bless generations, not just us individually. It is through entrepreneurship that we can facilitate a meaningful legacy in the financial arena, as well as the ability to give back, whether through philanthropy or simply giving back. God has given us the ability to leave a footprint on earth by the impact that we are able to make through this power called entrepreneurship and creating legacy.

God meticulously designed your uniqueness. Among the billions of people in the world, no two individuals share the same footprint. Everyone has a different footprint. Every person's legacy is distinguished by what they have been purposed and called to do. That becomes your footprint. Just as every fingerprint is unique, so too is each person's legacy or path in life. This uniqueness signals God's intention for us to understand that our legacy - what we are purposed and called to do - serves as our unique footprint in the world.

The presence of DNA or other forensic evidence at a crime scene helps to clarify who was involved in the crime. DNA evidence can be instrumental in linking an individual to the scene. The footprint of evidence is important in determining not just that someone was there, but potentially their role in the events that unfolded.

Your legacy, the mark you leave on the world, should be personal and unique to you. It should reflect your unique experiences, your life's mission, and your God-given purpose. This personal mission forms the essence of your legacy, creating a unique footprint that signifies your journey and contributions. The deliberate actions you undertake, inspired by your God-given purpose, amplify this legacy. The impact you make through these intentional acts becomes the mark you leave on the earth, proof that you existed and were present. It becomes your DNA.

## Legacy Matters Key #58

***You do a disservice to your family and community if you choose not to leave evidence of your existence on earth.***

Notable figures in history, like Dr. Martin Luther King Jr. and Harriet Tubman, are remembered not just because they existed, but because they left unforgettable marks on history through their deliberate action and commitment to their causes. Their footprints are evident because their living mattered. Their footprints are the lasting effects of their lives, which continue to influence us. Unlike these historical figures, many of us do not live with such intentionality, but the potential to do so remains within our reach. This legacy of impact invites us to consider how we can make meaningful contributions that endure beyond our lifetime.

You do a disservice to your family and community if we choose not to leave evidence of your existence on earth. You and I have a responsibility to make humanity better. Choosing not to leave a mark on the world is a missed opportunity to contribute positively to your family and community. When you opt out of making your presence known and felt, you forfeit the chance to influence your family and community in constructive ways, depriving future generations of the wisdom and legacy you could have imparted.

You should be conscious of how you spend your time, the choices you make, and the influence you have on other people and the environment. Creating your legacy entails defining objectives and setting goals to achieve personal and professional accomplishments. You have to be forward-thinking. You have to be clear about your goals and desires. You have to make sacrifices. You have to make a positive contribution to the well-being of other people, cultivating a feeling of community and working toward a society that is more compassionate and just. You have to be determined to live a life that makes family, community and humanity better. You have to give meaningful thought to what your life means in the present and after you die, because legacy is not just about dying.

The power of legacy is not only about enjoying the fruit of one's labor, but also watching your children's children enjoy the fruit of your labor. Many people erroneously view legacy as the footprint that they will leave when they die. But I want to declare very loudly that legacy is NOT just about death. The power of legacy is being able to see legacy lived out while you live.

## Legacy Matters Key #59

***Create with the end in mind.***

Legacy is like a relay race where you hand the baton to the next generation while you are yet living and breathing, and then sit back and say, "WOW!" Legacy is about your life, a life well lived and a life that is meaningful while you live.

***"Declaring the end from the beginning, and from ancient times the things that are not yet done, saying, My counsel shall stand, and I will do all my pleasure."***

***(Isaiah 46:10)***

God did not create a generation without thinking about the generations to follow. It is the nature of God to create with the end in mind. Therefore, since we possess the same characteristics of God to envision and plan with the ultimate outcome in focus, it suggests that we should approach our lives with the end goal in mind. There are no accidents or coincidences in the Bible. God is a God of purpose. Therefore, I believe that every event is created with the idea of Esther 4:14, *"For if you remain silent at this time, liberation and rescue will arise for the Jews from another place, and you and your father's house will perish [since you did not help when you had the chance]. And who knows whether you have attained royalty for such a time as this [and for this very purpose]?"* (Amplified Bible)

When I plan an event, I never plan the event from beginning to end. My approach is unconventional. I plan from the end to the beginning. This approach allows me to envision everything in the middle and account for all the intermediate steps. Think about it. If we embrace the nature of God and understand this vital characteristic of God, that He begins with the end in mind, then we can apply this principle to how we plan and live our lives. We are born to make a difference and our difference is our legacy.

**Take Charge**

***"God blessed them: "Prosper! Reproduce! Fill Earth! Take charge! Be responsible for fish in the sea and birds in the air, for every living thing that moves on the face of Earth." (Genesis 1:28, Message Bible)***

In Genesis 1:28, God commands Adam to "prosper, reproduce, fill the earth, take charge; be responsible for the fish in the sea and the birds in the air…" We have been given the power and authority to act and make decisions; but coupled with this power and authority is the obligation of responsibility. The emphasis is on responsibility. This power does not guarantee automatic success or progress. This brings us back to the concept of living intentionally.

We are commanded to take charge, which involves taking control, stepping up, doing our part, taking the initiative, and being proactive in our approach. The message is clear, you must actively manage your life. Your journey through life and your impact on the world will not happen by itself. The process is not on autopilot. You have to take charge and consciously steer your course. That is the powerful part of legacy.

## Legacy Matters Key #60

***Only you can do what God created you to do.***

If you are going to fill the earth and make your mark on the world, you have to take the initiative to leave that mark on record and in the earth. You have to take charge. Your leadership is non-transferable. No one else can do this for you except you. It is a task uniquely designed for you by God, tapping into your distinct capabilities and potential. This ties into the concept of DNA - only you can do what God created you to do. Therefore, take charge! Assume your role with confidence. Stand up in it. Walk in it. Be it.

*"Be responsible for fish in the sea and birds in the air, for every living thing that moves on the face of Earth."* Not only do you have to take charge, but you must also be responsible. This call to responsibility signifies not just the authority and dominion granted to us, but it also highlights the expectation of stewardship. The message is clear: Stop looking for other people to do what

God created and called you to do. You have the responsibility to understand the role you are to play in filling the earth and building your legacy.

Instead of focusing on the generations that fell short or the ones you believe might be irresponsible and mishandle what you leave for them, concentrate on being responsible for what God has assigned to your hands. One of the reasons people do not think about intentionally building their legacy is they don't want their children to squander what they worked so hard to achieve. This view can lead to a cycle of inaction, justified by the belief in the irresponsibility of the generations to follow (a sentiment I've admittedly shared myself). Avoid dwelling on past generations that failed to fulfill their duties or anticipating possible irresponsibility of future generations. Your responsibility is to actively manage the responsibilities God entrusted to you.

# Legacy Matters Key #61

***Take charge!***

Part of taking charge involves ensuring that all your legal matters are in order, a responsibility not to be taken lightly.

**Allow me to share another part of my story…**

*I know many entrepreneurs who have done philanthropic work. It has always been my desire to be remembered as someone who left on record a significant, meaningful contribution. With this goal in mind, I have been very intentional about my actions. My wife and I were asked by our attorney to come into his office to sign some documents. We initially thought it would be a quick visit. However, it turned out to be a significant moment where we finalized our last wishes, setting up trusts and taking care of other important legal matters. While we were in the office signing the documents, I felt a strange feeling of excitement come over me – Oh, my God, we did it!*

*There were two attorneys present and a few witnesses. The attorneys read aloud the various statements and clauses to which we had to agree. It was an impactful experience. One of the witnesses became visibly moved by the proceedings. I found myself feeling somewhat emotional as well. It was a monumental step. We had taken charge. It was more than just signing the documents. It was an emotionally charged realization that we had taken a significant step in building our legacy.*

*My wife and I are the generation that took charge. We organized our affairs, giving us a sense of readiness and preparedness. There is still much life ahead of us, yet this moment held an unexpected significance. Despite often speaking and teaching about the importance of legacy building, experiencing it firsthand brought a relief that our affairs are in order, arranged to reflect what is important to us and potentially impactful for those we have influenced. If anything were to happen to us now, we could rest easy knowing that we have taken proactive steps to secure our legacy. Our community will recognize the efforts and intentions behind our actions.*

*Reflecting on how I was going to build my legacy impacted life, the process was real. From the moment I made the decision to build a lasting legacy, every flight I took felt daunting because we had not finalized the legal documents yet. It is unfortunate, but I had allowed myself to be overtaken by the fear of dying before getting all my affairs in order. Despite actively working on it, the realization dawned on me that a simple Last Will and Testament hardly sufficed for the aspirations we hold and the greater ambitions we pursue. This incomplete task influenced my feelings towards travel, casting a shadow I did not understand until now. However, completing the process and signing the documents brought a sense of relief and release. We took charge and we got it done.*

**Life is Legacy**

What is life? What purpose does living serve? What drives the way you live your life? Why do you do what you do? Life is legacy. Your existence forms the foundation of your legacy. If we are true to ourselves, we will find that the thing that motivates us, the thing that keeps us going is not what we do for ourselves. Our actions are motivated by causes that are bigger than our personal desires and aspirations. These causes lay the groundwork for our legacy. Whether through philanthropic efforts aimed at impacting a specific area of life or through other means, what we leave behind goes beyond the end of our existence. Your legacy is defined not only by the outcome of your life, but the difference you make while you are living.

Everything you do (big, small or mediocre) ultimately plays a part in your legacy. Often, we do not view our daily actions through this lens, focusing on immediate needs rather than the lasting impact. However, every action contributes to the legacy you are creating for your family and community. The memories created during these times will leave a lasting impression, good, bad or indifferent.

# Legacy Matters Key #62

***Wealth building and legacy go hand-in-hand.***

While we may not always consciously think about building a legacy with our actions, this perspective is worth considering. How will my actions today impact my children, grandchildren, and great grandchildren? Oftentimes, we pass down traditions without knowing the reason for their origin. Have you heard statements like, *"That's what we've always done."* Whether it is the Howards, Smiths, Browns or your family, we do it because somebody, somewhere, somehow, started something. Whether through deliberate intention or by happenstance, these traditions form a legacy, embedding themselves in our family's narrative and shaping our identity. This cycle emphasizes the importance of being aware of the legacy we are creating with every action.

One of the challenges that I see is a possible shift in perspective about wealth building, especially in the framework of creating legacy. Many people are becoming more aware of the need to bridge the wealth gap, acknowledging that they have been left behind in terms of wealth building. Wealth building and legacy go hand-in-hand. Many people desire wealth but fail to understand how wealth leads to a lasting legacy for the family. They have selfish reasons for desiring wealth. It is evident by ways in which some people spend their money. Many people are still bigger consumers than they are producers.

Remember, it is my belief that every generation must make a sacrifice for the next generation, but there is one generation that must make the ultimate sacrifice - their lives. Therein lies the challenge with wealth building and legacy. The good news is, you have the power to amend your perspective and to determine your future and legacy. The choice is yours.

# CHAPTER SEVEN:
# FINANCIAL MATTERS

***"But thou shalt remember the LORD thy God: for it is he that giveth thee power to get wealth, that he may establish his covenant which he sware unto thy fathers, as it is this day." (Deuteronomy 8:18)***

**What's In Your Hand?**

Let's reflect on the practices of the Jewish community. Their actions resonate far beyond their lifetime. If you engage in a conversation with a Jewish person concerning wealth building and legacy, they are likely to attribute their success to their deeply ingrained values. I have a personal rabbi who gives me spiritual guidance. He shared with me an important lesson about the Jewish tradition. He shared, when Jewish entrepreneurs establish major institutions like hospitals and significant landmarks, they create more than just structures. They bring their children to these institutions and teach them a valuable life lesson. They tell their children, *"This is your is your starting point, your ground floor. You have to continue building the family legacy. The expectation is for you to go beyond this."*

This perspective sets the expectation of surpassing the achievements of the past. It is perhaps one of the reasons why the Jewish population is one of the smallest but wealthiest people groups.

## Legacy Matters Key #63

***Regardless of your financial status, organizing your financial affairs is critical.***

Financial planning, money management, and wealth building play a significant role in creating a lasting and powerful legacy. Understanding the importance of intentionally managing personal finances can lead to more informed decisions about wealth building and legacy planning. It will also help you determine what you consider valuable and guide you in aligning your actions with these values.

Financial matters are essential to think about. No one should desire to leave a financial burden on their family at the end of their life. Regardless of your financial status, organizing your financial affairs is critical. Whether you have significant wealth or very little money, it is imperative to get your financial affairs in order. Simple steps, such as securing a burial policy, can alleviate stress for your loved ones by ensuring there are funds allocated for funeral and burial expenses and final arrangements.

Establishing detailed financial plans, including wills, trusts, and other instruments, can protect your assets and ensure that your wishes control the distribution of your estate, and not the state. This is particularly important, as the state might otherwise dictate asset distribution through probate if your financial matters are left unresolved. It is also important to define the financial legacy you wish to establish. This will influence how you navigate life. It will give meaning and purpose to your actions and financial decisions. The key is intentionally managing your finances, driven by the desire to provide for your family.

## Legacy Matters Key #64

***Together, you and your family should be intentional about financial matters and wealth building.***

The reality is we all work for our families. Together, you and your family should be intentional about financial matters and wealth building. There should be discussions and conversations around wealth building, where your children and grandchildren and other significant family members are given the chance to give suggestions as to what they could do to build wealth. Suggestions for wealth-building could be practical. For example, investing in real estate is widely recognized as a substantial means of creating wealth and ensuring family financial security. Defining what it means to leave one's family financially secure is an intricate part of this process. Essentially, it involves thoughtful financial planning and decision-making that align with your legacy goals.

Consider the family home that a grandmother purchased for $60,000, that is now fully paid off. If she left that property for her children or family members to inherit, it could provide a substantial financial head start for them.

In some cases, the value of the land alone could surpass the value of the home itself. The problem is the grandmother may not see the significance of her home being paid in full. Many seniors have overlooked this asset. I have read reports where seniors have been taken advantage of by selling their homes for what appears to be a substantial amount, say $300,000, only to later learn that the actual value was much higher, perhaps even double.

***"And the Lord said unto him, What is that in thine hand? And he said, A rod." (Exodus 4:2)***

Many people fail to recognize what is in their hands and the power of it. They underestimate the value of what they already possess. In Exodus 4, God tells Moses to use what is in his hand so that the people would know that God was in their midst. In 2 Kings 4, God asked the widow woman who needed a financial breakthrough, "What do you have in your house?" The woman identified that she had nothing except a pot of oil. God then commanded her to borrow other vessels and demonstrated that when she used what she had, the oil miraculously multiplied, satisfying her financial need. The little became much. These stories are reminders to us to acknowledge and use even the seemingly insignificant resources we possess.

# Legacy Matters Key #65

***Start with what you have and be intentional.***

Sometimes people fail to recognize the "oil" they have right in their house. Start with what you have and be intentional. In practical terms, many people do not have their basic end-of-life arrangements in order, including life insurance, funeral arrangements or the money to cover these expenses. Some might think it is too late to take out an insurance policy at their age. However, by being proactive and exploring other creative solutions, it is still possible to significantly impact the legacy you want to leave behind. Take your time and research the cost of funeral services and related expenses. If you become proactive and intentional, you will find that your actions will transform your perception of your legacy and the state in which you leave your family when you leave this life.

**What Do I Need/Where Do I Start?**

As you are planning your financial legacy, there are five things to bear in mind:

***Life Insurance***

As mentioned earlier, at the very least, you should have a life insurance policy to cover your funeral and final expenses so that you do not leave that financial burden on your loved ones. If you currently do not have life insurance, I suggest you make this your first step.

My recommendation is to have life insurance coverage that is equal to six to ten times your annual salary until you reach a point where you are financially independent. For example, if your annual income is $100,000, acquiring life insurance coverage ranging from $600,000 to $1,000,000 is advisable. This amount ensures your loved ones a six to ten-year cushion to sustain the same standard of living based on your yearly earnings. Be very mindful to clearly designate your intended beneficiaries and delineate the distribution of your assets.

Things change in your life when things change. Therefore, it is also important to make sure your insurance policy/policies are up to date. For example, if a person was married and then divorces and remarries, they should make sure their life insurance policy reflects their wishes. They may choose to remove the ex-spouse from the policy and add the new spouse as the beneficiary. If this is overlooked and one of the spouses dies, the spouse named on the policy as beneficiary will legally have control of those monies. Many people fail to give thought to this.

Consider the basic expenses involved in organizing a funeral. It is important to reflect on these costs as they can guide your decision on the amount of life insurance coverage you may need. Expenses can include the service itself, the church or venue holding the services, potential costs for a wake or memorial gathering, and other arrangements. Reflecting on this helps you understand the financial aspect of your legacy. Your final farewell is a significant event, and the way it is conducted leaves a lasting impression. Ensuring you have the means for a fitting goodbye is part of the legacy you leave behind and it plays a role in how you are remembered.

***Bank Accounts***

It is very important to designate those who are authorized to access the funds in your bank accounts after your passing. This involves careful planning and understanding the various options available for designating beneficiaries or legal successors. By taking the appropriate steps, you can ensure that your assets are distributed according to your wishes, providing clarity and security for your loved ones. There are several methods to manage this, each with its own set of rules and implications. Thorough consideration is required to make informed decisions. Appointing an executor or someone who will carry out your instructions about your financial matters is a vital step to take in terms of your financial affairs. Ensuring that your financial intentions are clearly outlined for those you wish to inherit or receive your assets is vital.

***Money Management***

Money management is the process of maximizing your financial resources through intentional strategic decisions around budgeting, saving, investing, spending and overall usage of your financial resources and assets. Money management ensures the financial well-being of your family. Every financial decision you make is a steppingstone toward or a detour away from building wealth and a lasting financial legacy that spans generations.

Money management includes how you manage your money in each season of your life to support your family's goals and ensure their financial well-being. If you have children and/or grandchildren, consider the financial resources you can develop for their benefit. You can provide them with the ability to take control of their own financial future by providing them opportunities to mold their own future through the assets that you pass on to them.

To ensure that your assets are distributed in the manner that you wish, it is essential to specify your intended beneficiaries. Appointing an executor or someone who will carry out your instructions about your financial matters is a vital step to take in terms of your financial affairs.

***Own Nothing But Control Everything***

Steven Pollan and Mark Levine, authors of *Die Broke*, share a powerful financial planning strategy that I believe is key in building a long-lasting legacy. "Own nothing but control everything." I personally suggest transferring your possessions out of your name into a trust as you enter the age bracket of 50 to 55 years old. This proactive step is to safeguard your assets against possible medical expenses that could arise from unexpected health issues. By doing so, your wealth is protected from being depleted by high healthcare costs. There is a five-year lookback period, which means that any assets not placed in a trust within the five years prior to setting up the trust can be claimed to cover your medical bills. Financial assistance may be contingent upon the liquidation of your assets. Therefore, this strategy of owning no assets but maintaining control over them is vital.

Many individuals consider creating a will to outline their final wishes, not recognizing that establishing a trust may be a more advantageous option. While wills are subject to dispute in probate court, trusts are not, offering a more secure way to ensure your wishes are honored. Further details on this topic, including the distinctions between wills, trusts, and broader estate planning strategies will be explored in the Legal Matters chapter later in this book.

***Asset Management and Investments***

Asset management and investments are key in building wealth. Focusing on various investment vehicles such as stocks, bonds and real estate and exploring how these can be leveraged to establish a lasting financial legacy can significantly add to your financial portfolio. Historically, notable wealth builders like the Rockefellers, the Vanderbilts, and more recently, Warren Buffett, have utilized these exact investment strategies to accumulate significant wealth. This approach has been a tested pathway to wealth building, emphasizing the importance of gradually building wealth over time, rather than seeking a single, large financial gain. This method demonstrates a strategic and sustained effort to grow assets and secure a financial legacy.

It is especially important to have a skilled certified public accountant, a reputable broker, and an experienced estate and tax attorney on your team. They play a pivotal role in shaping your financial portfolio, ensuring that your financial goals are achieved within the legal boundaries. Their collaborative efforts are essential not only for managing your current financial affairs but also for providing a comprehensive understanding of your financial portfolio, which becomes particularly valuable in the event of your passing. Together, they ensure that your financial plan is executed seamlessly, safeguarding your legacy and ensuring clarity for your financial future.

**Little By Little**

***"Little by little I will drive them out before you, until you have increased enough to take possession of the land." (Exodus 27:30 NIV)***

Some people get frustrated with building wealth because they want to amass wealth in very large increments at one time, rather than gradually. They cancel themselves out of the wealth building game because they do not have large sums of money to invest, sums that will yield millions in one transaction. However, adopting a step-by-step approach with a strategic and patient mindset can yield significant results over time. The "little by little" approach will allow you to implement a strategy that is more effective over time. Start with a small amount that is manageable and then leverage the power of compound interest. Contrary to the belief that a large investment is required, incremental but consistent efforts build substantial wealth. By the time you look up, you will have amassed much more than you expected. The secret: little by little!

## Legacy Matters Key #66

***The goal in managing your finances is to enhance your net worth by reducing liabilities, while simultaneously leveraging your assets.***

You can start with as little as $50.00 a month. While it may not seem like a lot of money, over an extended period of time (30 years), the growth is remarkable, often exceeding your expectations. This methodical accumulation is a common strategy among those who have successfully amassed great wealth, utilizing the financial vehicles we discussed earlier (stocks, bonds and real estate).

At the end of the day, it is your assets versus your liabilities that determine your net worth, the difference between what you own (assets) and what you owe (liabilities). The goal in managing your finances is to enhance your net worth by reducing liabilities, while simultaneously leveraging your assets. It is the balance of assets minus liabilities that establishes your net worth, highlighting the critical role of effective debt management.

My personal financial journey began with a strong commitment to eliminating debt, placing me on the road to where I stand today. Initially, my focus was solely on being debt-free, as I believed that it would lay the foundation for future wealth accumulation. However, I learned that as you accumulate wealth, strategic debt can actually prove beneficial. There is a season you will have to work to minimize your debt, which gives you the capital you need to build wealth.

# Legacy Matters Key #67

***As you move the wealth needle you will need debt to offset taxes and liabilities.***

There comes a point where, after having reduced your debt to a manageable level and built up sufficient capital, leveraging controlled amounts of debt can be instrumental in building and sustaining wealth. This is an important aspect of my overall philosophy regarding debt and wealth management.

***"To every thing there is a season, and a time to every purpose under the heaven:" (Ecclesiastes 3:1)***

To everything there is a season. Therefore, understanding the season of life you are in has everything to do with how you work through managing debt and building wealth. In one season of my life, it was important for me to manage and get out of debt, because it allowed me to get the capital needed to move the wealth needle. Then at a certain point in my life, I recognized that I had moved to a place where I needed debt to offset my tax liability. However, I still had to manage the debt. There is "good" debt and "bad" debt. Debt that services itself and reduces your tax liability is good debt. Bad debt does not generate value or contribute to your net worth increase.

**Giving Matters**

From a financial perspective, giving matters. It is important to recognize the significance of giving and being charitable in living and upon death. The bottom line is money has a purpose. The purpose of money is not just to pay bills. Its true purpose extends far beyond covering expenses. The purpose of money is to cultivate a spirit of giving and to become philanthropic in this lifetime. That should be one of your goals. There is evidence to suggest that giving triggers the release of endorphins in the brain, which explains the joy we feel when we give. The capacity to be generous is important. In my view, and within my tradition, a baseline for giving could be setting aside at least 10% of whatever you generate to contribute towards greater causes. I firmly believe this act of giving does not just benefit others; it also enhances your own financial wellbeing.

It is very important to understand the impact and importance of the principle of giving. It has been a cornerstone of my teachings and personal practices. Giving changed my life, and I would be neglecting a key belief if I did not emphasize its significance. Giving is not just about how much money I have been able to give. My contributions extend beyond monetary donations.

As landlords, my wife and I have had the privilege of supporting families in acquiring their first homes. This role allows us not just to collect rent, but also to offer support during challenging times. Many of our tenants were about to be evicted due to nonpayment of rent, but my wife and I were able to help them stay in their homes, providing them with stability and another chance at life.

## Legacy Matters Key #68

***The purpose of money is to cultivate a spirit of giving and to become philanthropic in this lifetime.***

Giving encompasses more than just financial assistance. Being in a position of financial strength does more than just enhance your own life. It empowers you to support others in meaningful ways that might not have been possible otherwise. One of the most fulfilling aspects of being a landlord is the opportunity to offer individuals and families a chance to start anew and to shield them from homelessness. This act of kindness is what I see as offering them another chance at life. My wife and I have been committed to offering housing options to people with felony records who would otherwise face significant challenges in securing a home. In Tennessee, the barriers to renting with a felony record are substantial, making it difficult for those with felony records to find property owners willing to rent to them.

We have also provided support to seniors on fixed incomes, offering them financial assistance and opportunities. That is giving. Oftentimes, a person's giving goes unnoticed or unmentioned until after they have died, largely because these acts of kindness are not usually topics of public discussion. They are known mostly to the recipients of their generosity. My wife and I have assisted so many people over the years that we have actually lost count. Our approach to giving is not about keeping a tally. It is rooted in the belief that giving is inherently the right thing to do. We give because we know that giving is right.

Reflecting on our journey of support and kindness, I am reminded of the numerous instances where we have made a difference in people's lives. It brings to light the substantial impact we have made, often without even realizing the full extent of our contributions. Our commitment to charity and giving has extended beyond our role as landlords. It was also evident during the 20 years we operated our daycare. We encountered numerous families unable to afford the tuition and fees. We provided free or reduced tuition to many families, particularly for single mothers. We adjusted the fees to enable their children to attend a private daycare that was recognized as one of the best in the county.

# Legacy Matters Key #69

***Giving matters.***

There are many ways that you can give that does boil down to dollars and cents. However, it is not simply about handing out money. It is about providing valuable opportunities and support to those in need and filling a void, because giving matters.

According to Fidelity Charitable, *"A philanthropist is a person who donates time, money, experience, skills or talent to help create a better world. It emphasizes that philanthropy is not exclusive to people with considerable wealth or status. Anyone can be a philanthropist, regardless of status or net worth."* There is no requirement to donate large sums of money to be recognized as a giver. You do not have to give millions of dollars to be considered philanthropic. Philanthropy (giving) is a financial matter that is key in building a powerful legacy.

**Family Dynamics**

The way we approach financial legacy, inheritance, and the distribution of wealth is shaped by our family dynamics, cultural background, and the environment in which we were raised. Many people are not taught about money and money matters. This leaves a void in fully understanding the value of money and its proper use. You can only do what you know. This lack of knowledge often results in poor financial management.

Many of us have seen money being mishandled, misused, and mismanaged by the people we know. It is challenging to adopt sound money management practices without positive role models that demonstrate what it means to have good money management practices. I did not have these role models when I was growing up. Many people are still trying to find their identity through designer brands and luxury items.

I did not grasp the importance of managing finances until well into adulthood, at which point I was able to educate my own parents. Environmental and cultural influences affect how you see, understand, and handle money. Think about the multimillions of dollars that have passed through the United States government and where we are as a nation.

## Legacy Matters Key #70

***Environmental and cultural influences affect how you see, understand, and handle money.***

You have to be cognizant of where you come from and what you come from, and then start to transform your mindset regarding financial management. This shift in mindset involves understanding and being very clear about your goals in terms of wealth creation and financial objectives. It requires setting financial goals and devising a plan and a strategy to accomplish them. Everyone should desire to support their families and create wealth and impact for their children, grandchildren and great grandchildren. It is part of our creative nature.

The Bible says Abraham was rich, Isaac was wealthy, and Jacob was blessed. There was a progression of wealth. This reflects not just an increase in material wealth, but a cultural understanding of prosperity. This raises the question: should our focus be on the financial traditions of our own families, or should we align ourselves more closely with the principles found within the kingdom of God?

The kingdom of God has a blueprint for money and how to manage our finances effectively. Your family culture (meaning your family dynamics) matters. But while the influences of our family backgrounds are significant, it is important to recognize, for those who identify with being part of God's family and kingdom, that the kingdom perspective is the overriding guide. It offers a blueprint for how to responsibly handle and steward the resources we have been given.

Consider the current state of our nation. Some cultures, such as Hispanic and Asian cultures, place a strong emphasis on family values. These values, once deeply cherished in our own societal norms, such as the importance of extended family living together, continue to thrive within Hispanic, Asian and other communities. This silent yet powerful commitment to family legacy is evident. It is remarkable to observe the support system among these cultures, where multiple families might share a single home, pooling their resources to purchase it. This communal effort does not stop with one household. They continue this support, helping the next family to secure their home. This practice not only reinforces their strong familial bonds but also illustrates a practical approach to building and sustaining community and legacy.

# Legacy Matters Key #71

***The kingdom of God has a blueprint for money and how to manage our finances effectively.***

Other cultures struggle with the concept of shared living, often emphasizing the importance of independence and establishing one's own household as a mark of success. This is a mindset I am actively addressing with my children, challenging my own perception and considering alternatives. My wife prompted me to question the norms we have accepted. What if the widely accepted approach isn't the only way? Who said that children are supposed to grow up, move out and figure it out on their own, versus staying at home and establishing a strong financial foundation and then purchasing their own home. Who said that is the way it is supposed to be?

This has led me to explore different models, including kingdom principles on family and legacy. The necessity of this reevaluation has become more apparent as the cost of living soars, affecting young adults significantly. It is 2024, and my 30 year-old daughter works two jobs and still finds it difficult to afford an apartment on her own, highlighting the financial pressures faced by younger generations trying to live independently in today's economy.

Why do your children have to grow up and move out, particularly if you have the space to accommodate them? Somehow we have been made to believe that that is a sign of success – moving out and doing your own thing. Maybe the gift is to be able to assist your children for a period of time so that when they do leave, they do not have to rent an apartment. They can purchase their first home or first townhouse or their first piece of property.

Convincing children of the value of living at home can be challenging, especially in a society where independence is highly valued. However, the rising cost of living has made this option a necessity for many.

**Let me share another piece of my story to help illustrate this point...**

*At the time of the writing of this book, our youngest son, youngest daughter, and oldest daughter still live at home with my wife and me. It was important for me to help them understand that living at home does not equate to them being a failure. It is a blessing from God that allows them the opportunity to stay at home, and save and plan for the future in a supportive, loving family environment. This adjustment required some effort on my part. I had to work through it and change my perspective, especially with my son, because he is a male and I thought he needed to go through the process of finding his independence. He enjoys the independence and comfort of living in the apartment-style setup we have for him at home. It is almost like he has his own apartment in the lower level of our home, with his own private entrance. That is legacy building.*

*This realization made me think differently about our situation, recognizing the importance of setting boundaries and ensuring that this arrangement aids their growth rather than hinders it. It was important to establish some guidelines for them to follow – manage your finances responsibly, demonstrate accountability, and work towards your personal goals, just to name a few. I wanted to ensure that their stay at home was a steppingtone to their future success and not a setback.*

- ***What are your personal goals?***
- ***What are your financial goals?***

*I had to ensure that they understood that living at home isn't a free pass to irresponsibility or aimlessness. It is part of a deliberate strategy, a plan we were all in agreement with and actively pursuing. As long as everyone worked the plan, we were good. This strategy was about building legacy, offering support not just for the sake of giving support but as a tangible part of our legacy. It was giving while living, not after we died. That is part of the gift. That was part of our legacy.*

*If they viewed our assistance as a negative, they would miss the powerful lesson about legacy – that legacy is about what you do when you are living, as well as when you leave this life. Instead of seeing it as legacy, they would see it as "creating a limp," for them. However, it is not about enabling dependency (creating a limp), but rather about providing a boost ("giving a lift") towards achieving independence and success. Changing my perspective changed the entire meaning and value. Instead of viewing it with disdain, influenced by social norms that value individualism above family support, we learned to appreciate and enjoy the opportunity for growth and legacy building.*

*In addition, there was a season that my middle son and his wife lived with us for a year. This arrangement allowed them to save enough money for a downpayment on their home, a significant step towards financial independence. Unfortunately, I did not communicate the significance of this gesture effectively at the time, and they may not have recognized it as part of their legacy or fully valued the gift we gave to them. They could have felt entitled to it, like it was what we were expected to do as parents. This oversight highlights the importance of clear communication about the intentions and benefits behind such support.*

*My goal in sharing some of my experiences is to clarify the value of these acts of support not as obligations, but as gifts meant to give our children a lift in life. When my son and his wife later sold their home, they benefited from substantial equity they had gained after two years in their home, an outcome directly linked to the initial support my wife and I provided. This was not just about the initial financial help for the downpayment that they received as a result of living with us, but also about setting them up for a better future, an important part of our legacy. However, it remains a powerful example of the lasting impact of giving a lift, not just a gift.*

The support we provided to them was not free. It is easy to overlook that because as parents we often do things for our children without expecting anything in return. We tend to take these actions for granted, not fully recognizing their significance even to ourselves. But helping your children understand the magnitude of your support is important. It is still giving, even to your own children, and it is a form of philanthropy.

Once children become adults the support continues but the financial weight is greater - higher utility and food bills, for instance, which they may not have noticed. They assumed things were taken care of because they were living at home. Oftentimes, your children do not fully realize this or convey to others just how much they have been blessed by your support. This can contribute to a sense of entitlement, especially when they see what you have and assume they have a right to your assistance.

# Legacy Matters Key #72

***Legacy is not a debt owed to others. It is a gift given freely.***

It is not about what you owe to someone else, but what you owe to yourself. At its core, legacy is about your own story, your purpose, and how you wish to be remembered. The recipients are beneficiaries of what you have been called and created by God to do. Viewing legacy in this light, it is a blessing rather than an entitlement. Legacy is fundamentally about you, not just about those who receive it. Allowing our children to live in our home is not an obligation. It is part of the legacy I chose to create. We do it because we care about their future, providing a lift, not a limp. This distinction is paramount to building legacy.

If your children perceive it as a lift, their lives gain new meaning. Conversely, if they view it as a limp or if others mischaracterize it as such, it can damage your children in ways that can be irreparable. Their peers may criticize them, saying, *"You're 22 and still living at home?"*

*I often tell my children that many of their friends would envy their situation. My son's living area in the lower level of our home is larger and better equipped than most apartments he could rent at his age. He has the convenience of a private entrance through the garage into a space complete with a living room and kitchen, luxuries not typical for someone his age. This setup is part of the living legacy I am proud to witness.*

# CHAPTER EIGHT:
# **FAMILY MATTERS**

***"For whoever does the will of my Father in heaven is my brother and sister and mother." (Matthew 12:50)***

**Generations Matter**

What significance does life hold without the presence of family? Family infuses life with meaning, as it was conceived by God Himself. Everything God created He created with family in mind. Our actions are often motivated by family, extending beyond the ties of blood to those with whom we form deep connections and regard as family. We do not get to choose our relatives, but we do get to choose our family. That is how important family is to God.

## Legacy Matters Key #73

***Legacy is created while living.***

Family provides us with a sense of purpose and belonging. Our actions are driven by the idea of family. However, my definition of family goes beyond kinship to include those we consciously decide to include in our circle. For instance, many people refer to their church community as their church family, finding within it bonds that may surpass their biological relatives. Some of them are more like sisters and brothers than their biological siblings. The choice in who we consider family echoes the words of Jesus when he posed the question, "Who is my family?" He defined family as those who follow the will of God, suggesting a broader and more inclusive understanding of what constitutes family.

***"Know therefore that the LORD thy God, he is God, the faithful God, which keepeth covenant and mercy with them that love him and keep his commandments to a thousand generations." (Deuteronomy 7:9)***

God thinks generationally. He is a generational God. His vision spans across a thousand generations. There is a pattern throughout scripture that demonstrates that God is very much about legacy. Generations are important to God.

In Genesis 17:5, God promises Abraham, *"Nor shall your name any longer be Abram [high, exalted father]; but your name shall be Abraham [father of a multitude], for I have made you the father of many nations."* This pattern we see in the Bible speaks to legacy. It suggests that we should think generationally, looking beyond just the present generation to the broader expanse of time and lineage.

Legacy is created while living. As stated in Matthew 22:32, *"God is not the God of the dead, but of the living."* Your legacy is created during your lifetime, not after you leave this life. Once you are gone, you can no longer influence how you will be remembered nor intentionally build your legacy. God can help us in our living to accomplish those things that we desire to accomplish.

## Legacy Matters Key #74

***God is capable of bringing to fruition whatever you trust Him to do in your life.***

The decisions about your legacy must be made while you are alive. This is the essence of creating a living legacy. What you do with your life is what matters. Thus, you must ensure that your life has a meaningful impact. Every decision matters because every decision has consequences. God is capable of bringing to fruition whatever you trust Him to do in your life. He has the power to help you realize your desires while you live.

Consider what He accomplished for Abraham, Isaac, and Jacob as evidence of His ability to manifest your desires and aspirations. As we discussed in the previous chapter, the Bible notes that Abraham was rich, Isaac was wealthy, but Jacob received the Blessing. This indicates a pattern of generational growth, suggesting that with each generation there is an expectation of increase. Abraham's richness and Isaac's wealth were surpassed by Jacob's Blessing, which was limitless, highlighting the limitless potential available to us as heirs of God. Our life and living should extend well into our future, touching generations that have yet to be born. The question is how does your life and living impact generations to come?

Understanding the eternal nature of God and realizing that we share the very same nature, our perspective should not be confined to survival within our generation. Instead, we should consider how we can enable future generations to flourish, whether by building upon existing foundations or establishing new ones. It is important to remember that every generation must make a sacrifice, but one generation must make the ultimate sacrifice, which is to begin the journey of helping generations see and understand that legacy does matter.

Each generation should ask the question, "What will be my contribution to my family's legacy?" But then there is a generation that makes the ultimate sacrifice, creating the foundation and fundamental principles concerning legacy and its significance. This action ensures the continuation of your legacy beyond just one generation, fostering a lasting impact that supports and guides the generations to follow. Again, a good man leaves an inheritance for his children's children (Proverbs 13:22). As you intentionally build your family legacy, you should think generationally.

## Legacy Matters Key #75

***Each generation should seek to give the advantage to the next generation.***

Think about it - if every generation thought at least two to three generations ahead, the impact would be perpetual. The idea is to instill the same principles in every generation, maintaining a consistent focus on the concept of legacy across generations. This involves teaching the principles and strategies of wealth building and educating each generation about the level of sacrifice required to grow the family's wealth, ensuring it does not cease in your generation. How do we do this? Again, love always seeks to give the advantage. Each generation should seek to give the advantage to the next generation.

***"A good man leaves an inheritance [of moral stability and goodness] to his children's children, and the wealth of the sinner [finds its way eventually] into the hands of the righteous, for whom it was laid up."***

***(Proverbs 13:22, Amplified Version)***

A good man is a righteous man. It is part of the nature of a righteous man to invest in the wellbeing of his children's children and generations beyond. Our righteousness encompasses more than just our spiritual lives. It includes how we manage the affairs and responsibilities of our families. Therefore, understanding that a righteous person leaves an inheritance for his children's children is very important. This principle emphasizes that true righteousness is right living, which includes thinking generationally in terms of your life choices. How can you be a righteous man and not think about generations? A righteous man/woman must think generationally.

**Think Generationally**

***"The LORD said to Abram, after Lot had separated from him, "Lift up your eyes and look from the place where you are, northward and southward and eastward and westward, [15] for all the land that you see I will give to you and to your offspring forever. [16] I will make your offspring as the dust of the earth, so that if one can count the dust of the earth, your offspring also can be counted. [17] Arise, walk through the length and the breadth of the land, for I will give it to you." [18] So Abram moved his tent and came and settled by the oaks of Mamre, which are at Hebron, and there he built an altar to the LORD."***
***(Genesis 13:14-18)***

So, how does one think generationally? If you are going to think generationally, you have to look beyond yourself and your own generation. The Hebrew meaning for Lot is "cover or veil." Abram's vision was obscured as long as Lot was with him. It was only after they parted ways that God instructed Abram to look as far as he could see in every direction, promising him all the land within his sight. Despite the impossibility of the task, God told Abram to walk the breadth and length of the land that God was going to give to him. Yet, God commanded him to take the first step of the journey to becoming the father of many nations.

## Legacy Matters Key #76

***Thinking generationally influences every decision you make.***

How did Abraham envision becoming the father of many nations? How did he perceive us, given that we are his descendants and part of this legacy?

You and I are the seed of Abraham. This is about understanding your place as part of Abraham's lineage. In viewing the nations as God promised him, how does Abraham reconcile this vision with his reality? He must look beyond his immediate situation and surroundings, focusing instead on what God assigned him to do. Abraham is required to envision the future nations he is told he will father.

Thinking generationally requires us to do the same as Abraham. Look beyond your current world into the future and envision what lies ahead for the next generation and beyond, looking at one generation at a time. Start by considering the legacy you desire to create and build one generation at a time. What goals and aspirations do you have for your children? Then extend your vision to include your grandchildren and great-grandchildren and think about the impression you want to make on them and the impact you desire to have in their lives. Establish guidelines that can last beyond your grandchildren, provided they adhere to the plan.

My wife and I have put measures in place that will live beyond our grandchildren, if they follow the blueprint that we have established. Their success is contingent upon following this blueprint as it has been proven effective when applied correctly. Thinking generationally influences every decision you make. Every action you take will impact future generations - good, bad or indifferent - even something as simple as how you choose to spend your money.

## Legacy Matters Key #77

***The most effective lessons are those demonstrated through action.***

**Allow me to share a bit more of my story to illustrate this point…**

*The last time we bought Christmas gifts for our children was when my youngest son was six years old, which, as of the writing of this book, was over 16 years ago. As I mentioned earlier, Christmas was a major event in my family when I was growing up. My mother had a very large family, and she would buy gifts for everyone, her children, siblings, their children, and more. She spent a substantial amount of money each year on Christmas gifts, money that she could not afford to spend. This pattern of excessive spending became a pivotal lesson in my life. For years, my wife and I continued this tradition, mirroring my parents' behavior by celebrating Christmas on a grand scale, spending money that we really did not have. Eventually, I realized that this practice was detrimental to our financial health, which was a turning point for me.*

*I made a pivotal decision that we would not celebrate Christmas in the conventional way, specifically choosing to forego exchanging gifts. Naturally, this decision was met with disappointment from my children who were young and loved Christmas. We informed our family and friends that we would not be exchanging gifts anymore. I informed my parents, who were not happy, especially my mother, who still loved Christmas as much as she did when I was a child. I explained to my wife and children that we would use the money to pay off debts instead, aiming to secure our financial future. Despite initially feeling guilty and doubting my decision, I remained committed to this new course.*

*This disciplined approach paid off. We managed our finances with intention, which allowed us to eventually eliminate our debt. After clearing our debt, we improved our credit, ventured into buying real estate, and began building our assets significantly. A few years ago, I had the privilege to share this story publicly and reflect with my parents. During this moment, I reflected on the financial freedom we achieved, and said to my father, "I wonder how many people build their parents a million dollar wing on their house debt-free?" Well, we did for my parents. Out of that dysfunction came a discipline that ultimately brought deliverance to the whole family. To this day, we are able to take care of my parents because of that difficult decision.*

*We changed our approach to Christmas. The shift was not just about altering a holiday tradition but was rooted in a broader realization of its impact across generations and our journey towards financial freedom. Initially, my focus on changing our Christmas tradition was a means to get out of debt and provide a better life for my family. At that point, I was not thinking about my grandchildren and great grandchildren. My goal was to raise our standard of living so that we did not have to live paycheck to paycheck. So, I was ready to make the necessary sacrifices to achieve this end.*

# Legacy Matters Key #78

***In order to grasp the significance of intentionality in building your legacy, you must be goal oriented.***

Every decision moves you towards your goal or away from your goal. In order to grasp the significance of intentionality in building your legacy, you must be goal oriented. Adopting a mindset that spans generations starts with imparting financial wisdom to those in your immediate circle, including family and community members. Financial literacy is key. But it is more than just instruction. Set an example for them to follow. I believe the most effective lessons are those demonstrated through action.

My perspective on celebrating Christmas led my whole family to perceive Christmas in an entirely different light. Their upbringing has caused them to see Christmas differently. The challenge is in leveraging the insights gained from these experiences to deliberately build a strong legacy. As our children became adults and matured in their thinking, it was important for us to enhance our efforts and reinforce the "why" behind our actions. Again, thinking generationally. They are aware of what we did when they were young because they experienced it firsthand. Yet, I realized that we had not reiterated the purpose of our actions.

Now that they are adults, we had to clearly articulate our why. Initially, we made it clear to them the rationale behind our choices. However, it was necessary for me to revisit and re-explain the reasons to remind them why we diverged from the traditional way of celebrating Christmas. Our why was so that they could enjoy the fruit of our labor and the benefit of our sacrifices today. This was done not just for immediate gains but for the sustained well-being and enjoyment they have been experiencing over the years.

# Legacy Matters Key #79

***Examine where you spend your discretionary funds.***

This method is not limited to Christmas. Every family is different, and what works for one may not suit another. Examine where you spend your discretionary funds. Can these expenses be redirected towards investments that contribute to your family's long-term well-being and financial growth? This is not about ceasing to celebrate holidays and family milestones or altering traditions just for the sake of it. It is not about copying a specific action but about identifying what you are willing to adjust or forego to advance your family's goals. It is about thoughtful allocation of resources to build a legacy, setting priorities and making decisions that align with the legacy you desire to build. It requires more than a one-time change. It is a continuous practice of focusing on actions that yield perpetual benefits for generations to come.

Families often celebrate occasions like birthdays in traditional ways, but there is an opportunity to infuse these celebrations with deeper meaning. Instead of gifts that quickly lose value, consider giving a gift that keeps on giving, something that appreciates over time, such as bonds or stocks. Instead of giving your child or grandchild a toy or a game system that loses its value over time, give something that has lasting value.

**The Gift that Keeps On Giving**

Family matters. Recognizing the importance of family often highlights the criticism men face regarding their presence and involvement. As men, we are given the responsibility of the head and the provider, tasked with the welfare of the family. Therefore, sometimes it will require sacrifices such as missing our children's events and activities to fulfill this duty because we are the providers.

There were significant moments I missed because family matters, and prioritizing my family's needs was essential. Although there were times when I missed significant moments and events, times that I wish I could get back, when I look at where we are today, I made those choices because family is incredibly important to me. Initially, my children might not have understood why I had to be absent from certain moments, but the motivation behind my actions was always the welfare of our family.

## Legacy Matters Key #80

***Make your financials count.***

In all of this there has to be a balance, although it can be a challenge at times. I am a good provider and have always made family my priority. Yet, there have been times when I chose to forfeit an opportunity or delay a project, or put my family before the church to ensure my family felt prioritized. Every decision I have made, even those that might not have seemed to put the family first in the immediate moment, were driven by the underlying principle that family matters above all.

It is up to each family to decide their path. Each family should decide what they need to give up in order to meet the goals that have been set by the family. For some, it might be rethinking holiday celebrations, while for others, it might involve different sacrifices, like partying or going to restaurants frequently. Look and see where you are spending discretionary money that could go somewhere else and have much more meaning in life for the family. Make your financials count. Each family has to look within and see what they are willing to sacrifice. What am I willing to sacrifice for the next generation? The core principle is the same: consider the best ways to use your resources to support your family's future. Let your decisions be rooted in thoughtful goal-setting and long-term planning and it will eventually become the gift that keeps on giving.

Let's look at the Kennedy Family. Their deliberate and intentional wealth building strategies established a legacy that continues to benefit the Kennedy descendants for generations to come, ensuring they never have to worry about financial stability – **the gift that keeps on giving.**

Similarly, dynasties like the Vanderbilts and the Rothschilds have structured their legacies in such a way that even distant relatives benefit from their ancestors' foresight, wisdom and financial acumen. They built legacies that not only secured financial wealth but also ensured their names continue to be respected and remembered through time – **the gift that keeps on giving.**

How did they manage to create such lasting legacies that their names endure across generations? Without deliberate and intentional actions, many families witness their future generations squander wealth, leading to the dilution of their once-revered family names.

## Legacy Matters Key #81

***Legacy is not just about leaving, it's about living.***

Legacy is not just about when we die; it is about being able to see the fruit of our labor while we are living. Sacrifices will have to be made. Legacy is more than just preparing for the end of life. It is about living a life that aligns with the values we embody and wish to pass on. It is about creating a life that coincides with what you have modeled while living.

My desire is to not only leave a legacy after death but also to provide a quality of life for my family while I am still alive. I want to be part of their journey towards achieving milestones like owning real estate, rather than just leaving an inheritance. It is about family. Enjoying these moments together is key in building legacy.

This perspective was influenced by a conversation with my doctor, who practices this philosophy with her child. She has only one child. She believes in giving her daughter everything her daughter wants while she can still witness the joy it brings, rather than withholding it for a future date. Her perspective was, *"It is hers anyway, so I might as well watch her enjoy what is hers while I am living."* This exchange highlighted for me that the true essence of legacy is in seeing its benefits come to fruition during our lifetime, ensuring our affairs are arranged so this legacy continues even in our absence.

**A Good Name**

Legacy is not about individual achievements or material success. It is rooted in understanding and acting upon a shared purpose that transcends generations. The calling and purpose of God is not for just for the patriarch and the matriarch of the family to fulfill. We are called by God as a family. Together we are called to fulfill a collective calling and purpose, building a legacy that is about more than individual or immediate family achievements. It is about fulfilling a higher purpose that benefits communities and future generations, which is the foundation upon which the family's legacy is built. This shared purpose can manifest in various forms - ministry, business, or other contributions to society.

## Legacy Matters Key #82

***The spirit of legacy lives beyond your generation.***

**Allow me to share a little more of my story…**

*As I was raising my children, I had to make them understand that we are called by God as a family unit to build a powerful legacy. They had to understand that being a Howard is more than just a name. It is a calling, and as much as they may want to diverge from ministry, we were created for this purpose. It is not just an individual calling but one that encompasses the entire family, whether it relates to ministry or business.*

*My ancestors were remarkable entrepreneurs, even though I personally did not have the opportunity to know them. All I have are stories that relay their success in business during times when it was uncommon for Black people to own businesses. I see my own business successes as a continuation of this legacy. That is the spirit of legacy.*

The spirit of legacy lives beyond your generation, affecting not just the immediate generation but many generations to follow. My ancestors are looking from the balcony of heaven and rejoicing, celebrating the continuation of their legacy. The goal is for future generations to look back and acknowledge the foundations laid by their ancestors, something I aim to continue through my own legacy. You are creating legacy every day by the steps you take or refuse to take.

***"Now the LORD had said unto Abram, Get thee out of thy country, and from thy kindred, and from thy father's house, unto a land that I will shew thee: [2] And I will make of thee a great nation, and I will bless thee, and make thy name great; and thou shalt be a blessing: [3] And I will bless them that bless thee, and curse him that curseth thee: and in thee shall all families of the earth be blessed. [4] So Abram departed, as the LORD had spoken unto him; and Lot went with him: and Abram was seventy and five years old when he departed out of Haran." (Genesis 12:1-4)***

Abraham was already rich and well-established before God called him. In Genesis chapter 12, we witness what can be likened to Abraham's spiritual rebirth or initiation into a new life with God. This moment marks Abraham's entry into God's kingdom, symbolizing a transition from darkness to light, a pivotal point that highlights the significance of understanding one's divine calling. God emphasizes the importance of legacy by promising to make Abraham's name great.

# Legacy Matters Key #83

***Your legacy is tied to your name and the impact it has in the earth.***

God made a covenant with Abraham, promising to make him a great nation, to bless him, and to make his name great so that he could be a source of blessings to others. This is the essence of legacy: the capacity to be a blessing to others. This divine directive was given to Abraham, the patriarch of our faith, marking us as descendants of his lineage.

In verse 4, the Bible notes that Abraham was 75 years old when he departed Haran. It took another 25 years for Abraham to see the fulfillment of God's promise, illustrating that one is never too old to realize God's promises. This interval between the promise and its fulfillment served as a maturation period, a period of growth and preparation. God's initial pledge to make Abraham's name great depicts the connection between your reputation and legacy. It was not just about Abraham becoming the father of many nations, but it was the distinction of his name being made great. Your legacy is tied to your name and the impact it has in the earth.

The Bible says a good name is rather to be chosen than great riches (Proverbs 22:1). In the Old Testament, names were very important. There was deliberate intent behind the naming of children. Legacy is about your name.

# Legacy Matters Key #84

***What makes your name great is how you bless others.***

What comes up when people hear your name? What you deposit in others determines how great your name will be, not how much you accumulate for yourself, not how much people say you had when you die. It is what you do with what God has given you. What makes your name great is how you bless others - *"Thou shalt be a blessing."* So, when you hear about the people who leave a lasting legacy, the ones who make a real mark are those who have established foundations and demonstrated a willingness to sacrifice and give for the benefit of others.

I once read a story about a janitor who sponsored numerous students through college despite his modest income. This was not by chance. He made a deliberate choice. He was intentional because of his commitment to making a difference. He was not a business owner or top level executive. He did not have millions of dollars. Yet his story illustrates that impactful legacies are not exclusively the domain of the wealthy. Even with limited resources, you can significantly influence the lives of others. His name is great because of how he blessed others.

Think about it. Every official document you sign is linked to your name. Your identity in the world and your creditworthiness are evaluated based on your name. While your Social Security number might seem like the key identifier in identifying who you are, it is still connected to your name. When you were born, you were given a name, and when you die, you are known by that name. From birth to death, your name is your constant identifier, which highlights why God's promise to Abraham to make his name great was so significant.

God assured Abraham that by adhering to His plan, his name would achieve greatness. Centuries later, we are still talking about Abraham, proving God's promise true. Abraham's legacy was not just about his own prosperity, but his legacy was defined by how he enriched the lives of others.

## Legacy Matters Key #85

***Legacy is about what you deposit in others.***

Names carry significant meaning. Allow me to share a bit more of my story…

*My name was not chosen by my mother because of its meaning. I was named Amos because my mother named me after my father. Yet it was on purpose in the eyes of God because my destiny is tied to my name. Amos means, "burden bearer." My biological father's name was also Amos. Although we did not have a relationship growing up, he served a significant purpose in my life. His role was pivotal in giving me my name. He played a role in shaping my divine purpose and my legacy.*

*Even when you are born into less than ideal circumstances or situations that are not favorable, when you think about who you are, whose you are (God), and what God has assigned you to do, remember that God uses it all for your good. All things work together for the good of them that love God and are called according to His purpose (Romans 8:28).*

*God is a purposeful God. He operates with deliberate intent. I have been able to reconcile with my biological father, recognizing his part in my story, without harboring any feelings of resentment toward him. This mindset stems from my conviction that ultimately, every experience will contribute positively to my life, a belief that has consistently proven true in my life. From a very young age, I counseled adults, offering guidance to both married and single people.*

*Surprisingly, many adults sought my advice and counsel, highlighting the impact of my name on my legacy. Again, a good name is more desirable than riches. Legacy goes beyond material wealth. This was the legacy of my ancestors. Although they did not have a lot of money, they had a good name that granted them trust and credibility, such as being able to obtain goods on credit at the local store based solely on their good name. All they had was their name and that was the legacy they left for us.*

*Reflecting on my own heritage, I come from a family named the Strongs, a name associated with integrity. My grandfather built a very large home by hand, where his children still live today. They did not have a lot of money, but what they did have was their name. This legacy of integrity and trustworthiness was what our grandparents relied on, rather than financial wealth or credit scores.*

Today, we witness a departure from valuing a good name to prioritizing material gain, a temptation not new to humanity. If you are not able to leave your children substantial wealth, it is important to make sure they inherit a respected name. Whenever an individual is in the process of building their legacy, challenges will arise, because life happens. You can proceed and even reestablish your name while continuing to build your legacy despite the setbacks. There is always a chance for redemption and the possibility to reshape how your name is perceived. That is called the grace of God.

# Legacy Matters Key #86

***God is a God of another chance.***

Many people have made mistakes that could have marred or shamed their name in some way. The key lies in taking full accountability for your actions and making amends in a way that demonstrates genuine change. This allows others to recognize your growth and transformation. We can see this in the story of Abraham. After deviating from God's path, Abraham experienced a period of silence from God that lasted 25 years. However, upon receiving a new understanding and aligning himself once again with God's will, Abraham was able to continue his journey, ultimately being remembered not for his missteps but as the father of many nations. God is a God of another chance.

There are things in my own life that I regret, but I hold onto the conviction that certain missteps can be overcome if you are willing to change your course. The potential for redemption depends on whether you can demonstrate change over time. You can outlive it if you live long enough. There is something about a name.

***"Wherefore God also hath highly exalted him, and given him a name which is above every name: 10 That at the name of Jesus every knee should bow, of things in heaven, and things in earth, and things under the earth." (Philippians 2:9-10)***

What is your name? What access does your name give you? Your name can greatly influence the opportunities and access you have in life. Philippians 2, highlights the power of the name of Jesus. This passage of scripture shows the impact and authority in the name of Jesus. When the name of Jesus is mentioned, it suggests the vast legacy of his deeds and teachings. The life of Jesus is a reminder of the powerful connection between your name and your legacy.

# Legacy Matters Key #87

***Your name can greatly influence the opportunities and access you have in life.***

Sometimes the family name you inherit may not carry the legacy of integrity or significance you desire to carry. Perhaps the reputation of your ancestors has tarnished the family name. I believe in the transformative power of grace that enables you to redefine that legacy. In everyone's generation there are actions taken by those who are the patriarchs/matriarchs that may bring into question the family name.

By the grace of God, we are given the ability to shift the narrative of how people view our name starting with our actions. This grace does not excuse their actions but allows for a new chapter where our name is associated with different, more positive contributions. This change not only alters the legacy for our generation but also extends its benefits to our ancestors in a way, covering them under a new light of grace. What you are able to accomplish covers the family name.

This concept extends beyond individual families to cultural traditions and practices. The desire for a male heir, for instance, is often about continuing the family name rather than a preference of a gender. The issue of women hyphenating their names upon marriage can be seen as controversial, reflecting deep-rooted beliefs about family identity and legacy. When a daughter marries, the emotional moment for a father symbolizes not just a transfer of care but also the passing on of the family name. It raises the question of whether the new family name can uphold and honor the legacy it carries. I advise my daughters to consider if a potential partner can meet or exceed the standards set by their upbringing, not necessarily in material terms but in the capacity to provide and uphold the dignity of the name. The power of a name is profound, embodying not just identity but a legacy of actions, values, and expectations that can be carried forward through generations with intention and grace.

# CHAPTER NINE:
# HISTORY MATTERS

***"Again Jesus spoke to them, saying, "I am the light of the world. Whoever follows me will not walk in darkness, but will have the light of life."*** [13] ***So the Pharisees said to him, "You are bearing witness about yourself; your testimony is not true."*** [1] ***Jesus answered, "Even if I do bear witness about myself, my testimony is true, for I know where I came from and where I am going, but you do not know where I come from or where I am going." (John 8:12-14)***

**Where Did You Come From?**

History is more than just a series of events. It is the chronicling of your story. It is a narrative that belongs to each of us. History is your story, your experiences, your background, the backdrop of your life. Therefore, it is essential to understand your history.

## Legacy Matters Key #88

***Your family history will give insight into who you are and where you come from.***

The journey into our family history often reveals how our present lives are connected to the legacy left by those who came before us. This journey often reveals patterns, values, and traditions that have been passed down through generations, influencing our decisions and shaping our futures in ways we might not even realize. Delving into your family history is not just learning what happened in the past. It is discovering how these events contribute to your personal story and identity.

Some people argue that learning your family history is important so that history does not repeat itself in your life. However, everything in your history is not a bad thing. There are certain aspects of your history that you may want to replicate. Understanding your family history is important in comprehending the true essence of your family's legacy. What does your history mean to your family?

The more you understand your family history and its significance to your family and the generations to follow you, the more clarity you will have about who you are, your purpose, and the purpose God entrusted to your family lineage to accomplish on this earth. This knowledge will strengthen your connection to your roots and help you better understand your role in carrying on the legacy of your family. Your family history will give insight into who you are and where you come from.

Reflecting on Jesus' words, in John 8, He confidently stated, *"I know who I am, and I know where I come from."* Jesus' words emphasize the importance of understanding both your identity and your history. There is great value in knowing your background and the inner strength that resides within you. In moments of weakness or discouragement, reflecting on your history can provide immense strength. Jesus' life exemplifies this truth. When faced with pressure, Jesus was not compelled to conform because He was secure in His identity and His history.

## Legacy Matters Key #89

***Your family history is not just a record of the past but a tribute to your lineage, strength, and potential.***

History gives you the opportunity to reflect on where you came from. Your family history is not just a record of the past but a tribute to your lineage, strength, and potential. Understanding who you are and where you come from is a game changer.

To begin exploring your history, I recommend starting with the elders in your family. For example, in our family we have a young man who serves as the family historian. He knows many of the stories about our family. He knows where our family came from. Find that person or persons in your family and begin to engage with them and document their insights.

One year, at my family reunion, we made a point to record the elders of my family sharing our family history. The interaction with the elders of our family was invaluable as they shared firsthand accounts of our family history. Listening to the stories they shared brought us closer together as a family. While there are numerous tools available for genealogical research, the firsthand experiences and stories from living relatives offer unparalleled depth.

Younger family members may not immediately recognize the value of these stories, but they illuminate our backgrounds in vivid and meaningful ways. Research programs can trace lineage and connections, but the stories from our elders add color and depth to our understanding, enriching our sense of identity and connection to our past.

If you do not know your family history due to adoption or other reasons, embark on your own journey of discovery about your origin. However, in the greater scheme of things, God orders our steps and guides our path. There are those who are adopted into families, and although they are not biologically connected, they become an integral part of their history. Their assignment aligns with the assignment of their adopted family. This is by divine design, aligning with a greater purpose and assignment.

## Legacy Matters Key #90

***God orders our steps and guides our path.***

**Allow me to share a bit more of my story…**

*I was not raised by my biological father. I was raised by my stepfather. My biological father was not involved in the church, but the man who raised me was deeply spiritual and a preacher and helped shape my path to becoming the preacher and pastor I am today. This shift in my upbringing was divinely orchestrated by God.*

*While I do not believe God orchestrated the divorce of my biological father and my mother, I do believe He works through all circumstances for the benefit of those who love Him and are called according to His purpose. This divine intervention has guided my life towards a path it might not have taken under the care of my biological father. God works things in our favor even when we do not recognize it. Even in this, God still had legacy in mind based on my creative purpose.*

Have you ever heard the saying, "What happens in this house stays in this house?" This is a common saying in many families. This saying highlights the numerous unresolved challenges, issues, and concerns present within families. These unresolved issues often become the "pink elephant" in the room that no one wants to address. If not addressed, unresolved issues can negatively impact your family's legacy.

It is very important to address both the family business and the silent issues that often linger within the family, aiming not for criticism but for understanding the foundational aspects that define the family. Despite any arising issues or challenges, being a part of a family holds significant value. Your family still matters. While some may choose to sever family ties for various reasons, family connections are very important in building a strong legacy.

**No Man Is An Island**

Some people do not see the significance of family. They focus on their personal achievements, goals and aspirations, living their lives with the mindset that family connections are not important. However, the importance of family cannot be understated. The concept of family is rooted in God. If family was not essential, we would have been created as solitary beings, each pursuing our own paths independently. We were designed to thrive within the framework of family. No man is an island. No one can exist in complete isolation. Our nature and purpose are intertwined with others. These connections are vital to our identity and our missions in life. They extend beyond our immediate family, encompassing those who support and assist us in our journey.

# Legacy Matters Key #91

***Success is not achieved alone.***

There is no "I" in success. Success is not achieved alone. It requires the collective effort and support of other people. Those who help us in our endeavors are part of our extended family. Family values and success strategies can be passed down from generation to generation. This is part of legacy building. As I look back on my own life, the value of hard work was passed down to me. I recognize the importance of diligence as a virtue instilled in me by my biological father, my mother's relatives, and the father who raised me. Hard work was a common thread among many of my family members, including aunts and uncles.

Entrepreneurship also played a pivotal role in shaping my life. I have been an entrepreneur for much of my life. As a teenager, I was always exploring ways to earn money. My entrepreneurial spirit was further validated when the elders of my family shared stories of how different family members, dating back to slavery, were entrepreneurs and the kinds of businesses they owned. Learning about my family history and the rich examples of business ownership, made me realize that entrepreneurship was not just a personal inclination, but a legacy handed down to me.

I also observed a unique value within my family emphasizing the importance of mutual protection. Despite any internal conflicts, there was an unwavering support system against external threats. We may fight amongst ourselves, but we would not let anyone outside of our family circle fight us. There was a sense of family unity and protection, which influenced my perspective on family values, instilling in me the importance of being the protector of my family. These experiences and the lessons learned from them have been instrumental in shaping the values I have and wish to pass on to my children, grandchildren, great grandchildren and beyond. I will do whatever I can to ensure that my family does not have to endure the same hardships I witnessed growing up.

## Legacy Matters Key #92

***No man is an island.***

Another core value instilled in me is the belief that a man should financially support his family. This perspective came with a narrow definition of support, emphasizing material provision but not the emotional and mental wellbeing of the family. I don't blame my parents for this limitation. I recognize that their ability to provide such support was probably constrained by their own experiences and lack of examples in this area. This approach granted my father a certain freedom to act as he pleased in other areas of family life. He believed that if he financially supported his family he fulfilled his role as a good man.

This inherited belief now challenges me as I navigate my own role as a parent. Despite a tendency toward workaholism, I am actively working to ensure I am not just financially responsible for my children but also present and supportive of their emotional and mental needs. It is vital for me to shift this aspect of the legacy I pass on to ensure that my children feel supported not only materially but also emotionally and mentally.

As we discussed in earlier chapters, every generation must make a sacrifice for the next generations to follow, but there is a generation that must make the ultimate sacrifice. Sacrifice is one of those values that must be passed down within the family for the benefit of the legacy of the family. The one who makes the ultimate sacrifice is the one who understands their identity, purpose, and the direction in which they should lead their family, aligning with the divine path intended for them.

While I recognize that there are those in my family who have made sacrifices along the way, my wife and I have made many sacrifice. We have been very intentional in our decisions and actions, be it financial or emotional, for the sake of our family legacy. We made a deliberate commitment to forego certain comforts for the benefit of the family. Why? No man is an island.

**Allow me to share another piece of my story to illustrate this point…**

*For about seven years, my wife and I opted to drive used vehicles that were within our means, choosing to pay for them outright. Our goal was to live debt-free. This decision often subjected us to ridicule and criticism from relatives and fellow church members. I was a successful pastor of a church, but I chose to own and drive a 1989 Chevy Corsica. Debt-free living was important to me, and driving that Corsica that I bought for $2,500 in cash, was proof. My choice of vehicles brought considerable pushback, especially from those in my church and family circle who found it bewildering. When my parents came to visit us, I had to use the church van to pick them up from the airport because their luggage could not fit into the trunk of our Corsica.*

*We sacrificed going on vacations, opted for secondhand goods over new, and even delayed furnishing our home when we first bought it. Our commitment to avoiding debt meant that our house had bedroom furniture but lacked furniture in the living and dining rooms. Gatherings at our home often involved sitting on the floor or using borrowed tables and chairs from the church because I refused to purchase furniture on credit. This lifestyle was a sacrifice, but it was one we willingly made, believing that forgoing certain comforts for a time would lead to greater enjoyment in future seasons of our lives.*

*We were the generation that made the ultimate sacrifice. Ultimately, we were able to maintain A1 credit. Our sacrifices opened opportunities to gain financial knowledge and literacy that radically changed our lives and enabled us to venture into buying real estate, which laid the groundwork for building a portfolio that included both residential and commercial properties. All of this came with a level of sacrifice that I had to commit to, but also my wife and my family. No man is an island. There were moments when even my immediate family, my wife included, found the sacrifices we were making to be quite daunting. There were times they couldn't grasp the reasons behind our choices, feeling frustrated and even angry with me for the decisions I made. But in the end it was worth it because we were able to establish financial stability and ultimately, create streams of income that enhanced our family legacy.*

## Legacy Matters Key #93

***Purpose outlives the sacrifice.***

Sacrifice should always be made with purpose. The sacrifice is for the greater good and purpose of the family. My motivation was to provide a life for my family that was free from the hardships my parents faced. This fueled my determination to do better.

I believe many people share this aspiration for a better life for their families, yet not everyone is prepared to undertake the necessary sacrifices to achieve it. The question is, are you willing to make the sacrifices? According to Dennis Kimbro, in his book, *What Makes the Great Great*, *"What makes the great, great are the sacrifices that one is willing to make to fulfill what they have been purposed to do."*

**Health Matters**

***"Beloved, I pray that you may prosper in every way and [that your body] may keep well, even as [I know] your soul keeps well and prospers."***

***(3 John 2, Amplified Version)***

Beyond financial and material sacrifices, there are critical non-monetary sacrifices essential to legacy building, notably emotional and mental ones. Many people find themselves trapped by the emotional and psychological burdens from their past experiences. These emotional sacrifices are necessary. Without them many people risk clinging to past traumas and dramas, hindering their ability to contribute positively to their family's legacy. Every family has dysfunctional dynamics that demand a significant emotional investment to navigate these challenges.

Your mental, emotional and physical health are key factors in building a strong and powerful legacy. What lies at the core of your being? What aspects of your life do you wish for others to understand and acknowledge? People often equate their significance to their possessions or accomplishments, but you matter because God created you. Since you matter, then there are actions that you must take to maintain your health and wellbeing. This includes nurturing your mental, physical, spiritual, and emotional well-being.

Many people neglect their own needs because they are caring for others, often resulting in a decline in their own health. Many have suffered or passed away sooner than necessary due to neglecting self-care. The aspects concerning your well-being - THE MATTERS OF YOU - deserve attention. Your health should take precedence. What is wealth without good health? What is legacy if you cannot enjoy the fruit of your labor while you are living? You must prioritize what matters to you.

## Legacy Matters Key #94

***The aspects concerning your well-being - THE MATTERS OF YOU - deserve attention.***

When it comes to maintaining your physical health, it is not just about rigorous exercise but also about regular health checks and maintaining your physical condition. This includes annual physical exams and taking proactive steps to address medical needs, ensuring you are in good health. Paying attention to your health is vital for leaving a meaningful legacy. Neglecting your health could lead to premature death, undermining your efforts to create a lasting impact. Are you giving any consideration to your health matters as you are thinking about creating legacy? Don't obsess over it but recognize that health is an essential factor in your legacy planning.

From my personal experience, had I remained fixated on the emotional and psychological harm inflicted upon me as a child, fulfilling my duties as a son would have been impossible. As you are crafting your legacy, you have to be willing to let go of some emotional capital for the sake of something greater. Letting go means choosing not to let the pain, trauma, and drama of the past weigh you down. Think about how many families and individuals are paralyzed because of the emotional and mental trauma that they may be experiencing or have experienced in the past, but do not know how to let it go.

The idea is not to make these sacrifices at your own expense, but rather to recognize when it is necessary to sacrifice it for the greater good of the family. We have all faced challenges within our families that can lead to the detriment of the family unit if not released emotionally and mentally. Many people suffer silently, and oftentimes it has to do with unresolved expectations that they have not been able to let go of. You must maintain mental fortitude and strength in order to be psychologically stable and resist life's difficulties and pressures. Unspoken expectations can be challenging. They occur when others hold expectations of you without openly communicating their expectations. I have had to personally overcome significant emotional turmoil for my family's sake. I have had to forego a lot of mental trauma and pain for the good of the family, often putting my own well-being on the line.

## Legacy Matters Key #95

***You must maintain mental fortitude and strength in order to be psychologically stable and resist life's difficulties and pressures.***

My journey toward healing led me to seek therapy, a step I took despite not initially believing I needed it. This decision was influenced by a friend who highlighted the benefits of talking to a professional, despite my own background in psychology and counseling and my skepticism about the need for therapy myself.

I have always supported the idea of therapy but never saw myself as someone who needed it, especially given my success in business. However, curiosity and a recommendation from a friend who had seen considerable benefits from therapy motivated me to give it a try. My friend advised, "If you do the work, it will work." His advice seemed abstract at first, but after two years of dedicated effort, my life significantly improved. I was willing to do the work and make the necessary sacrifices.

Concerns about the affordability of therapy are common, but you cannot put a price on mental health and well-being. Prioritizing and investing in your mental health is vital and the benefits of doing the necessary work are invaluable. The power of awareness is the power to change. Pursue the extent of help you require without allowing insurance limitations to interrupt your journey. This is about recognizing your worth. Consider this: when a household appliance fails, you somehow manage to find the resources to replace it. Yet, many hesitate to invest in counseling due to its cost, overlooking the importance of their well-being.

Remember, on this legacy journey, you matter. The expense we often dismiss as too high for counseling is frequently squandered on less significant things within a month. Weekly sessions may not be feasible for everyone. I encourage you to do whatever is necessary for YOUR well-being.

# Legacy Matters Key #96

***If you do not understand who you are, others will attempt to define you.***

Aiming to be the best version of yourself stems from acknowledging your own value. Sometimes to be the best version of you, you have to discover who you really are, which often involves navigating through layers of dysfunction, disappointment, and chaos. The real you is often tucked away in that. If you do not understand who you are, others will attempt to define you. Therapy and counseling will give you the most effective and comprehensive care you need. You are your greatest asset!

**The Maturation Period**

***"When I was a child, I spake as a child, I understood as a child, I thought as a child: but when I became a man, I put away childish things." (1 Corinthians 13:11)***

Everything God created goes through a maturation process, a period of development. Consider a seed. A seed embarks on an intricate journey to become what we eventually observe as the harvest of that seed. A tree does not transform into its full form overnight. There is a maturation period that you have to go through, a process of growth and development that should not be prematurely interrupted.

Oftentimes people want to abort the process and expedite growth because they desire immediate results. They want it quick. They have a "microwave" understanding of things, disregarding the fact that true legacy cannot be hastily constructed. Legacy is initiated and cultivated over the span of time you have been given on this earth. Legacy is intentional and deliberate.

Regardless of the duration of time we believe we are granted on this earth, each of us is destined to navigate through a specific journey. This journey involves discovering our true selves and grasping the purpose we are meant to fulfill. This is all part of the growth and maturation process, leading you to a place where the significance and power of leaving a legacy becomes crystal clear. I did not have this level of understanding a decade ago. My current outlook has been shaped by a series of life experiences that has brought me to the realization that my life is bigger than just living.

## Legacy Matters Key #97

***There is a maturation period, a period of growth and development that is inevitable for our lives.***

Life unfolds in a series of chapters. Sometimes we stop reading before we get to the next chapter. There are pivotal moments within these chapters of our lives that significantly contribute to our overall development into who God created us to be. This progression is evident in the transition from childhood to adulthood. A child does not remain a child indefinitely.

***"I have fought a good fight, I have finished my course, I have kept the faith: Henceforth there is laid up for me a crown of righteousness, which the Lord, the righteous judge, shall give me at that day: and not to me only, but unto all them also that love his appearing." (2 Timothy 4:7-8)***

In the above passage of scripture, Paul is saying, throughout my own journey, I have matured and gained insight and a deeper understanding of many aspects of life. From the moment of my calling, I've evolved significantly. This reflects a maturity and understanding that Paul did not possess at the beginning of his spiritual journey. Paul has to go through a series of life experiences that eventually move him to a place where he understands his purpose and God's plan for his life. But at the end of the day, Paul expresses, "If I die today, I am fine with it because I recognize through my maturation period I have lived a full life and finished my course." Reaching this level of understanding signifies the essence of the maturation process.

Paul's realization is a result of the experiences that led him to a state of readiness to "die empty," having fulfilled his purpose. In essence, he was passing the baton, which signifies the completion of his duties. Passing the baton does not mean that he has to die at that moment. It simply marks the fulfillment of his designated role. Paul transitions to a phase where he can appreciate the outcomes of his efforts and focus on guiding and advising those who continue the work he started, ensuring they are well-equipped to carry on the mission.

This is the essence of the maturation process, realizing that while life may seem to revolve around you, in the big picture it really doesn't. It is not about you. But then again, it is about you. It is a play on words. It is about you because it is your story, your narrative. Then again, it is not about you, because at the end of the day, it is about your assignment, your purpose, God's plan for your life. It is what you are supposed to do. Achieving this level of maturity brings a sense of comfort, recognizing that your purpose goes beyond just yourself.

## Legacy Matters Key #98

***True maturity comes from recognizing the value of your contributions and achievements that God has allowed you to achieve.***

This touches on the challenge of succession planning, which many people find difficult. The maturation period is coming to a place where you have the freedom to release control, rather than clinging to it until death due to a lack of foresight or preparation. True maturity comes from recognizing the worth of your contributions and achievements that God has allowed you to achieve, where you can comfortably pass on the reins - and you do not have to die to let go. Many people view this process as daunting, overwhelming, and complicated, uncertain of how to begin or doubting what they have to contribute.

That is not how your story has to end. Your story does not have to conclude on a predetermined note. Consider the account of the man at the pool of Bethesda in John 5. For 38 years he was identified as the crippled man residing at the pool of Bethesda. This was his legacy until his encounter with Jesus, who posed an important question to him, "Do you want to be made whole?" Upon his positive response, Jesus commanded, "Take up your bed and walk." The change had nothing to do with Jesus. The change had to take place within the man himself.

The bed represents the obstacles that stopped him from moving forward. The issue was not his inability to walk, but rather his comfort with the bed that immobilized him. Jesus aimed to help him overcome the barriers to his advancement. It is about shifting your perspective. Stand up and resolve that this will not be the conclusion of your narrative, nor how you will be remembered. Refuse to be remembered as the person who was stuck in their life. That may be where your story started, but it is not where it will end.

## Legacy Matters Key #99

***To build a strong legacy, you must make decisive moves.***

The responsibility for altering your legacy rests with you. You must seize your destiny. It is not the duration of your wait that defines you. If you want it, you have to take it. If you want to see change in your life, it demands personal initiative rather than expecting it to be handed to you. Many people express a desire for change, but they hesitate to act on it, waiting for others to facilitate their growth. To build a strong legacy, you must make decisive moves.

It is time for you to make a decision. No decision is a decision. It's not about leaving; it is about living. Make a decision - even if your credit is poor. Make a decision - even if your money is low. Make a decision. You are about to take a step that will steer you towards shaping your own story and building your legacy, ensuring it unfolds the way you desire. Take up your bed and walk! Your past does not dictate your future.

**How Do You See Your Story Ending?**

How do you see your story ending? Are you writing the script for your story, or is someone else writing the script? Are you being intentional about your actions, decisions and plans? Success is not an accident. Carve out some time to reflect on your life. Pause to evaluate where you stand at different milestones of your life. For instance, at age 55, one might ponder whether they are where they anticipated being and what they expect to accomplish by age 65, as life progresses.

Many people envision their story ending in terms of eternal rest, especially those with a faith perspective, imagining it as a transition to heaven. However, I believe you should experience heaven on earth, which for me means touching as many lives as possible. Striving to make a tangible difference affirms the significance of my existence. Envisioning my story's end involves not just looking forward to a heavenly reward but actively seeking to embody those values and impact in my earthly journey. It involves being able to really say that I made a difference and that my life mattered.

# Legacy Matters Key #100

***You are your greatest asset.***

Remember, you are your greatest asset. The way you manage and care for yourself directly impacts what you can offer and provide for your loved ones. Prioritizing your well-being is important, not just for your own sake but for your ability to support your family effectively. While it may not traditionally be viewed as a financial asset, your personal health and wellness are paramount.

Ensuring you undergo regular health screenings, maintaining your physical and mental health, and doing everything necessary to be in the best possible condition are essential practices. It is important not to limit assets to just financial instruments like stocks, bonds, or real estate. Recognizing and nurturing your personal health and wellbeing is equally, if not more important. So, how do you see your story ending?

# CHAPTER TEN:
# LEADERSHIP MATTERS

***"For as he thinketh in his heart, so is he." (Proverbs 23:7)***

**Legacy is a Mindset**

Everything starts with the mind. Mindset is essential in doing the basic mechanics of life. You cannot do the basic mechanics without the mind to do so. Mindset and mechanics go hand-in-hand. Many people struggle with the basic mechanics of life because they do not have the right mindset. They face challenges in their mind trying to overcome destructive tendencies that keep them from completing the important tasks in life. This also sheds light on why some people shy away from conversations about significant issues, such as planning for their affairs after death. This issue speaks directly to mindset, but many people do not talk about it. You cannot do the basic mechanics of life if you do not have the right mindset concerning your life and legacy.

## Legacy Matters Key #101

***Mindset has the power to shape your perspectives and decisions.***

According to a *USA Today* report in 2024, "More than 100 million Americans are uninsured or underinsured when it comes to life insurance."[1] This often happens because many people have the mindset that they have plenty of time left. There are also those who have the mindset that because they are single and have no children, they don't need life insurance coverage.

Mindset has the power to shape your perspectives and decisions. The challenge comes in your ability to break out of a limiting and self-sabotaging mindset and set the groundwork for a generational mindset, creating a new approach to thinking that will benefit future generations. The reason many people have not seen this type of transformation in their lives is because they have not made the effort to change, so the burden gets thrown on a family member. It is a vicious cycle that must be broken.

**Allow me to share a bit more of my story…**

*One action I have taken is securing insurance policies for my grandchildren. Initially, this required me to shift my mindset significantly because I had many preconceived notions, such as questioning the necessity of this type of insurance for them. However, my insurance broker explained the benefits not in terms of anticipating their premature death, but as a financial strategy. After making payments on the policy for a set period of time, the policy's face value can then be presented to my grandchildren at a certain age, as a gift. It essentially transforms the policy into a gift. That is a different mindset. I had to shift my perspective. The insurance can support their college expenses, among other things. It is all about adopting a different mindset, one that focuses on building generational wealth. There are numerous approaches to this, and securing insurance as a future gift for my grandchildren is a prime example of such a strategy.*

*For this specific insurance policy, my premium payments are minimum. For a minimal investment in my grandchildren's future, there is a significant return for the gift that is given to the next generation. Some people might argue that they don't have enough money to make the investment, but I am convinced that if they examine their spending habits, they will find they are wasting much more money than the minimal investment. It's all about mindset.*

## Legacy Matters Key #102

***You do not BECOME what you think; you ARE what you think at the time you think it.***

This is not to say you do not have the right mindset, but rather to encourage you to consider whether you have viewed life from this perspective. It is about fostering a completely new way of thinking. Adopting such a mindset not only changes your perspective but also generates a different energy, leading to a different vibration, which in turn initiates a ripple effect in your life, attracting the resources you need to achieve your goals. That is the power of the mind.

Proverbs 23:7 says, *"For as he thinketh in his heart, so is he."* You do not BECOME what you think; you ARE what you think at the time you think it. That is where many people miss it. That is the power of thinking generationally. Reflecting on the people God chose, God took them beyond their current circumstances and enabled them to envision possibilities far beyond their immediate perception. You can only manifest what you think to be so. In other words, you can only bring into reality what you believe is possible. This concept is central to the power of this book and its emphasis on the mental aspect of legacy creation. It is all about adopting a particular mindset. Once you truly internalize and mentally commit to the idea that your goals are attainable, they become reality.

**Be Intentional**

It is important to be intentional about legacy building, succession planning and passing the leadership baton. This is a very important step. Many business owners, entrepreneurs and ministry leaders overlook it. What actions should be taken when a successor has not been appointed?

**Let me share a bit more of my story…**

*I have chosen my son to succeed me in leading the church. However, at the time of writing this book, he is only 22 years old. We both need to be more intentional in preparation for this transition. If something were to happen to me in the coming year, there would be a void. Nonetheless, it is essential to ensure that everything is in order legally. I have laid out a detailed plan of what to do and I have already taken care of those details.*

## Legacy Matters Key #103

***Succession planning is vital.***

I firmly believe it is critical for pastors to engage in succession planning. I specifically want to address pastors here, since I am a pastor. There should be guidance available to help pastors understand their obligation to their congregations in navigating this process. It is astonishing to observe the number of pastors who have not thought about succession planning, some of whom have led their churches for 30 plus years.

I know of a pastor who pastored his church for over 40 years, but he preferred not to designate a successor. He wanted the church to choose the successor. I know of another pastor who has been in his role for 40 years. He engaged with his church to navigate the succession process but insisted on not swaying their decision. This approach is concerning because the pastor should have more say in the matter. This method does not align with biblical examples. Nevertheless, many pastors fail to recognize the necessity of appointing a successor to carry on the work that they so diligently built. This approach risks the possibility of the culmination of one's lifelong ministry fading away with their passing. Succession planning is vital.

There are some pastors who ensure their church affairs are managed well, but their personal affairs may not be as organized, particularly their home life. I know of several senior pastors who were regarded as successful because of their lavish lifestyles and the large sizes of their congregations. However, as they aged, a lack of planning led to financial hardship. One pastor comes to mind. He was once among the nation's leading pastors but after suffering a medical setback he faces significant challenges. Despite advice given to him during his healthier years about organizing his affairs, he failed to take action.

## Legacy Matters Key #104

***It's not about how long you live; it's how well you live.***

Consequently, his church declined and struggled to survive. The church's difficulties were compounded by the pastor's lack of retirement planning, leaving the church to support him and his family while also covering its expenses. Although he is still officially the pastor, an interim pastor has taken over his duties. This situation has persisted for years, and he has not stepped down. This raises concerns about the legacy he will leave behind and what could have been if he had prepared for his succession and properly passed the baton.

These same principles apply for business owners and entrepreneurs. At some point in time, everyone reflects on the entirety of their life. However, you may not frame these thoughts in terms of legacy, possibly because the concept of legacy is often tied to the accumulation of material wealth. The common perception of legacy tends to focus on the material possessions one can pass on, rather than recognizing its broader significance.

It's not about how long you live; it's how well you live. Jesus only lived 33 years, but look at the power of his life. Look at the impact and the legacy he left. Oftentimes when young lives are tragically cut short, it prompts people to question the impact those individuals managed to make in their brief time. But it is not about how long you live. It is about how well you live.

Consider a child who, due to health complications, lives only a short while - be it a year, six months, or even a month. The existence of the child carries a legacy. Their brief life greatly affects their parents, altering their outlook on life. This is the essence of legacy. While the child may be unaware of concepts like legacy or making a lasting impact, their presence significantly shapes their family's dynamic and leaves a lasting mark on their lives. Consider even a stillborn child. This tragedy becomes a defining part of the legacy for the parents. It alters their perspective on life, and demonstrates the profound effect a person can have on their loved ones, regardless of the length of their life. These examples illustrate the power in creating your legacy.

## Legacy Matters Key #105

***Legacy begins and ends in the womb.***

***"Before I formed thee in the belly I knew thee; and before thou camest forth out of the womb I sanctified thee, and I ordained thee a prophet unto the nations." (Jeremiah 1:5)***

Consider the example of the Prophet Jeremiah, as detailed in Jeremiah 1:5, where God states He knew and formed Jeremiah even before his birth, assigning his purpose early on. This divine intention granted Jeremiah remarkable authority and power at a young age. Similarly, Shadrach, Meshach, and Abednego were teenagers when they made significant contributions. My goal is to shift how you view your life and perceive your own existence.

Remember, the legacy you leave behind, whether good, bad or indifferent, is shaped by your actions and how you choose to live your life. It may not always be at the forefront of your mind, but ultimately, legacy reflects how you want to be remembered. What thoughts or images come to mind when people hear your name? Your legacy is continuously being crafted, which is why it is important to be intentional about how you narrate your story. To achieve the outcome you desire, it is essential to be deliberate in your actions and decisions. By "outcome," I am referring not just to the final chapters of your life but to the impact and legacy you desire to establish throughout your journey.

**Living Legacy**

Living legacy is not waiting until you die to see the fruit of your labor. Living legacy is being consciously aware that everything you do and every decision you make matters. Each choice you make carries weight. Legacy encompasses the way you live every day.

As I have shared in previous chapters, for years, I intentionally lived a very disciplined lifestyle financially so that my family could experience living legacy. My family is living proof that you can enjoy the fruit of your labor while you are still living. They are living right now in legacy. Everything I do is about legacy. Every action I take is driven by the desire to create a lasting legacy on purpose and in purpose. I am very intentional about making sure that my family experiences a life of legacy - and it is important for me to witness it.

## Legacy Matters Key #106

***Living legacy is important not only in your future decisions but in your present actions.***

Caring for my parents is a significant aspect of the legacy I value. My parents live with me. My wife and I had a 5,000 square foot addition added to our home to accommodate their needs. We essentially constructed a separate house on our property that is tailored to their needs. That is living legacy. It is a blessing to be able to take care of my parents. Living legacy is important not only in your future decisions but in your present actions.

I incorporate this principle into my ministry, ensuring that every action is deliberate and aligned with purpose. The sacrifices and commitments we make for the sake of our ministry are not by chance. They are thoughtfully chosen paths to fulfill our mission. Each decision and sacrifice is made with the intention of serving a greater good, underlining the importance of living and acting on purpose and in purpose in every aspect of our work. This ensures that our ministry not only achieves its goals but does so in a manner that is meaningful and impactful. Living legacy is living your life with the understanding that every decision that you make is made with legacy in mind.

**Passing the Baton**

In the context of legacy and leadership, passing the baton refers to the deliberate and strategic transition of knowledge, values, responsibilities, and leadership roles from one generation or leader to the next. It is very similar to a relay race where the baton represents the wisdom, knowledge, traditions, achievements, and vision of an organization, family, or community. This process ensures continuity and growth, allowing the successors to build upon the foundations laid by their predecessors.

Passing the baton involves instilling and transferring values, ethics, and lessons learned, ensuring that the core principles and ideals of the leader are preserved and adapted over time. It requires preparing the next generation to carry forward the mission and objectives with their own contributions and innovations, while maintaining the spirit and integrity of the original vision.

# Legacy Matters Key #107

***Effective leaders prepare for their transition by identifying and nurturing potential successors.***

They provide them with the necessary skills, experiences, and understanding of the organization's culture and goals. This ensures that when the time comes for leadership to change hands and the baton to be passed, the organization continues to thrive under new leadership. Passing the baton in this way is important for sustainable success and the impact of the leader's legacy. God always begins with the end in mind.

God does not bring anything into existence without envisioning its conclusion. There are people that God places in our lives specifically to assist us in achieving and fulfilling the objectives He has ordained for us on earth.

I frequently remind my children and family members that their place in our family was determined at birth, whether they like it or not. I firmly and lovingly remind them, "You were born into this!" In every family that God created and every individual within that family, there exists a unique DNA that carries the legacy and purpose God has intended. This purpose and the work that God has orchestrated for you to accomplish remains unfinished without someone to continue it. In other words, completing God's work necessitates having a successor to whom you can pass the baton, ensuring that the mission is carried forward and continued for generations to come.

# Legacy Matters Key #108

***Your family is a business.***

Legacy is not solely about a person identifying and pursuing their purpose. It also involves the responsibility to prepare and guide the next person in line. This ensures that successors understand the significance of their work and the essence of the life lived before them, enabling them to carry on the legacy effectively. Every person must find a person. Your family is a business. So, how do you carry on the family name? Who is going to be responsible? Who is going to be the next patriarch/matriarch to step up and lead? That is legacy.

It is very interesting when you consider the family dynamics of some families, how the matriarch and the patriarch of the family (figures some lovingly refer to as "Big Mama" and "Granddaddy") were well aware of this. But they instinctively knew it. Think about it, there is always one child in the family who the matriarch and/or the patriarch is harder on and has greater expectations of than the others. They are more strict with them; they expect more from them. This particular child is given greater responsibilities and often feels the burden of becoming the rock of the family.

The magnitude and the weight of the responsibility can be exhausting and at times overwhelming. Yet, it is often not until Big Mama or Granddaddy are nearing the end of their journey that the "chosen one" recognizes the assignment for which they were being prepared. They realize that all along they were being groomed to step into the role of the family's matriarch/patriarch. The selection of the person to take on this role is not limited by gender or age. It is a divine assignment given to the family leaders, which is why leadership matters.

# Legacy Matters Key #109

***Leadership matters.***

In my wife's family, her grandmother relied on her as the pillar of strength, despite my wife being younger than her seven uncles and aunts. Her grandmother turned to her, seeing a quality within her that prompted her to entrust the family business to her. Each generation must pinpoint someone to whom they can pass the baton, ensuring the continuity of their legacy. From a legal perspective, you should appoint an executor for your estate. This individual may not be the same as the one to whom the baton is ultimately passed, but they are entrusted with ensuring the baton reaches the right person to fulfill your final wishes. (More about this will be explained in the Legal Matters chapter.)

Every family is tasked with this responsibility, which extends beyond material assets. It is identifying the person whom the family's matriarch and/or patriarch deem most capable of preserving family traditions and sustaining the legacy.

**Leadership for Life**

Leadership matters within the family unit. Someone has to step up and take the initiative to build a legacy that is going to benefit generations to come. Someone has to be willing to step out of their comfort zone and take the risks that will ultimately result in generational wealth, health and wholeness. Someone has to be committed to initiate and lead discussions that shape the future of the family.

Everyone has the potential to be a leader, but the strongest leader is the one who can first lead him/herself. Leadership is more than just influencing others. Leaders should be able to envision the future. Leaders within the family must be able to communicate and shape the vision for the overall wellbeing of the family. True leaders live and lead from the future.

Plainly said, leaders lead. In contemplating legacy and legacy matters, someone has to take the lead within the family. Oftentimes, we wait for others to take responsibility for what happens in our lives, but the key is to lead yourself and take charge of your own destiny. By doing so, we lead with a vision for the future, embracing our responsibilities and the paths we are destined to follow.

# Legacy Matters Key #110

***Leadership is the ability to influence others.***

Leadership matters in creating legacy and it starts with you leading you. Before guiding others, you must first become the architect of your own journey. You are the first leader in your life tasked with grasping the reins firmly and steering your path. Leadership of self involves mastering your domain, taking control over your actions, and recognizing that self-governance is the key to advancement in life. To excel as a leader throughout life, you must take responsibility for your own life and your actions, and make deliberate choices to navigate your life effectively. No one can take care of you like you can. In building your legacy, you must take the lead because no one else understands the assignment from God regarding the purpose and destiny you are meant to fulfill quite like you do. Striving to be the best version of yourself can give rise to the advancement, growth, and prosperity you desire.

Leadership is the ability to influence others. When considering this within the context of family, recognizing your ability to affect change in others is important. It is important to understand the strength of your influence within your family and community. This influence extends beyond the words that you say. It is equally about your actions and how they inspire those around you.

Your influence has the power to change people for better or worse. From a legacy perspective, leadership has everything to do with empowering and influencing those who will inherit and contribute to what you will leave behind when you transition from this life. Therefore, you must communicate your legacy in a way that encourages them to embrace it willingly and with joy. The real power of leadership is not in compelling others to follow but in inspiring them to take joy in the journey, viewing it as a privilege rather than an obligation.

# Legacy Matters Key #111

***Striving to be the best version of yourself can give rise to the advancement, growth, and prosperity you desire.***

Let's explore some of the challenges people face when they take on leadership roles within the family to maintain and enhance their legacy.

1. **Lack of Confidence.** One significant challenge many people encounter is the daunting feeling that they cannot live up to the expectations of a role they have inherited. Some may say, *"Those are very big shoes to fill."* This sense of inadequacy can be overwhelming. Take for instance, the legacy of Dr. Martin Luther King, Jr. It is a daunting idea to continue what he represented, which often leads to the belief that one cannot measure up to such stature. Overcoming this mindset is important. The fact that you were chosen as the leader indicates that others believe in your capability. Many people see potential in you that you may not see in yourself.
2. **Lack of Resources.** Another challenge arises when someone in the family is tasked to continue a legacy, but they have doubts whether they have the necessary resources to sustain it. Some people may choose to quit, give in, or set aside the legacy when they feel resources are lacking. However, don't allow yourself to make excuses. Excuses are a misuse of your imagination. Where God guides, He provides. Do not focus on the absence of resources, but instead focus on finding ways to fulfill and continue the legacy.
3. **Feeling Unworthy.** Another challenge to overcome is the feeling of unworthiness. Oftentimes, our heroes who provide us with the succession plan for the family legacy can seem larger than life to us. In their shadow, it is easy to diminish your own self-worth. However, it is important to understand that they are not expecting you to be them. They are encouraging you to be the best version of you. There is something unique about you that qualifies you to continue the legacy. Many people struggle with the notion that they cannot surpass their heroes or the individuals they deeply admire. If not managed carefully, this mindset can lead to placing these figures on a pedestal above yourself and even above God. Maintaining perspective is essential.

4. **Inability to Live Up to the Name.** We discussed the significance of a name and its power. However, living up to a name can be intimidating for many. This concern often ties in with the "hero syndrome." If you carry a namesake, whether it be a first or last name, the expectation is not just to live up to the name but to continue adding and building upon it. What matters is your ability to enhance and expand the legacy associated with the name.

## Legacy Matters Key #112

***Failures are never final.***

Leaders must understand that failure is an integral part of the journey of life. The key is to shift how you view failure. If not understood correctly, failure can stop your progress. There is no failure in God. Reframe your perspective on failure. Although failure is a part of life, it is more about how we perceive and respond to it. I use failure as a learning curve, lessons learned that are never to be repeated. I learn what to do and what not to do. Failures are never final.

**Allow me to share a bit more of my story to illustrate this...**

*I remember working on a particular project for my business. Up until this point, I had consistently earned at least $100,000 on a project, which was an extraordinary achievement at the time. Even accountants and bankers were baffled by my success. I know it was the favor of God on my life that allowed me to achieve unprecedented results. However, for this particular project, I experienced a major setback. I lost more than $100,000. The loss was devastating for me. I was depressed, disappointed, and disillusioned about the whole transaction.*

*At first, I saw the loss as a failure, but eventually, I decided to change my perspective. This change in perspective was transformative for me and it gave me new life. Instead of seeing the loss of money as a loss, I began to describe it as a $100,000 lesson learned. I learned from the experience, choosing to see it not as a loss but as a gain. This mindset shift helped me move forward and continue doing the work that I do today. Most people see failure as a loss. I view it as an opportunity for gain.*

*If you change your perspective about failure from being something you lost - be it time, money, a job, relationships – you will find that you are able to move forward in some things that paralyzed you in the past. Failure tends to induce fear, and fear is immobilizing. It prevents us from achieving our potential and moving forward. Recognizing this, I changed how I perceive failure. Now, I don't see setbacks as losses. Instead, they are valuable lessons that fuel my progress.*

# Legacy Matters Key #113

***From a kingdom perspective, there is no such thing as loss.***

From a kingdom perspective, there is no such thing as loss. From a financial standpoint, where others might say someone has lost a certain amount of money in an endeavor, I see it differently. I don't see it as a loss; I see it as planting a seed. By redefining what might be considered a loss as a seed, I set the stage for future growth. After all, when you plant a seed, don't you expect a harvest? I have had projects that I invested in that were classified as unprofitable. My response, *"I never lose. That investment was a seed, and I anticipate a harvest."* This approach has proven effective repeatedly. While the results may not be immediate, I am confident they will manifest in time.

I have many stories that illustrate this point, but they all stem from changing my perspective on failure. What is your perspective on failure? Many people view their life or their legacy through the lens of failure, focusing on the setbacks they have encountered in their life. If that is you, you must change how you perceive those experiences. Those experiences are part of your story. They are part of your narrative. Those stories are part of what helps your legacy become more meaningful and powerful.

Every great legacy has encountered failure. Consider any historical figure that we deem as great or our heroes. If you examine their lives, you will notice periods marked by apparent failures, but if you revisit these moments, you'll see that their failures often paved the way for their most significant achievements. Think of the number of times Thomas Edison failed in creating the lightbulb before he got it right. Think about the number of times Michael Jordan failed before he became one of the greatest basketball players in history. Michael Jordan had far more missed shots than he did putting the ball through the hoop. Failure is not about loss; it is about learning and growth.

**Tough Conversations**

Death and dying are tough conversations. Many people do not want to have the tough conversations. It is amazing how many people avoid these conversations, even though everyone is aware that they will eventually die. There is a common belief that speaking about death might somehow bring it closer, as if verbalizing it could manifest it into reality. This is so far from the truth. Addressing mortality is essential, yet many families shy away from these discussions.

## Legacy Matters Key #114

***Regardless of how you feel, you must be willing to have the tough conversations about what happens after you leave this life.***

Another way to view the discussion of mortality is to see it as a means of ensuring your final wishes are fulfilled. It's all about perspective. According to my interpretation of scripture, we are promised 120 years of life (Genesis 6:3). There are examples where people have chosen their time of departure. Having a conversation about what happens upon my death does not accelerate my death, it enhances my living, because I can live with a new level of freedom. Knowing everything is arranged allows me to live from a different vantage point, a peace of mind that regardless of what happens, my affairs are in order.

Regardless of how you feel, you must be willing to have the tough conversations about what happens after you leave this life, even though everyone in your family may not be ready to engage in such mature discussions. Identify those in your family who are mature enough to have the tough conversations. For example, my youngest son is 22, and my oldest is 34. I had to have the tough conversation and inquire, "Have you considered what you would do in the event that something happened to your mother and I?" It is important to discuss various scenarios, such as the possibility that my wife may outlive me. If that happens, what support will they provide her? How will they manage our affairs?

My wife was involved in the legal aspects of our plans, and I put things in place to help guide her through the process. However, it is equally her responsibility to fully understand the legal arrangements. I explained to her that if something happens to me, she should follow specific steps to ensure that she maintains the lifestyle she is accustomed to, and who to rely on for support. Of course, we had our lawyer directly involved. Nonetheless, we had to have the tough conversations as a family. That is not to say the conversations were not difficult. At one point she said, "You aren't going anywhere." Well, no I do not plan on going anywhere, but the possibility is always there. Life is like a vapor.

## Legacy Matters Key #115

***Conversations alone are NOT legally binding.***

It is important to understand that having the tough conversations is just the beginning. The conversations alone are NOT legally binding. Many people discuss their wishes verbally, but fail to formalize these intentions through legal documentation. Consequently, when someone passes away, claims about their verbal wishes carry little weight if they are not supported in writing. Merely saying, *"He said he wanted to be cremated;" "She said she wanted her daughter to take over running the business,"* based on someone's verbal conversation is insufficient. I have seen many cases where verbal wishes were disputed or ignored because the conversations were not legally documented. While it is important to have these conversations, they must be followed up with legal action to ensure that any confidential discussions are solidified and recognized by law.

Many people keep emergency funds ("rainy day money") in their home. For our grandparents and great grandparents, having $5,000 to $10,000 on hand was a significant amount. It may not seem like much today, but it was substantial for them back then. My wife's grandmother and grandfather raised her as their own child. Her grandfather believed in keeping cash at home. My wife ultimately was responsible for managing their affairs. It is fascinating to see the dynamics of how children are raised and the responsibilities they ultimately inherit.

The tough conversations are necessary and important to have with your loved ones. There are many tough conversations to have, especially around procedures during grieving times. When a loved one passes away everyone is grieving. Emotions are high. That is not the time to try to figure out what your loved one desires. If the tough conversations are had while your loved one is alive, the process will be peaceful. Ideally, the details of the discussions should be clearly outlined in legal documents, like wills or trusts, to avoid any confusion or disputes. Once decisions are made, the successor should be named early enough for everyone to be aware, especially in roles such as a pastor or a business owner. People need to know the plans for future leadership and the handling of various responsibilities. These are challenging discussions, but they are necessary to ensure clarity and continuity within your legacy.

Gather as a family and begin to have the tough conversations, discussing the challenging topics. In my family, we refer to these gatherings as "family times of sharing," rather than just meetings. We come together as a family unit. This approach allows everyone to hear the same story and develop a shared understanding. Discuss funeral arrangements and expenses.

## Legacy Matters Key #116

***Tough conversations are necessary, as they ensure that your intentions for your legacy are understood and respected.***

As of the writing of this book, the average cost of cremation is $7,000. The average cost of burial is $15,000. Today, many funeral homes will not perform the burial rites of your loved one until they have received payment. It is important to gather the family together to ensure everyone is on the same page. This does not necessarily mean delving into the specifics of who inherits what, but at least sharing your overall wishes. Sometimes it may be necessary to discuss specific details. The important thing is to start gathering the family and having the tough conversations as soon as possible.

I also had to engage in tough conversations with key leaders in my ministry and business as I formalized legal documents concerning my ministry. I told one of my key leaders that I needed to speak with them because I trust that they would uphold my wishes should anything happen to me. I emphasized that I am doing everything possible to ensure that my wishes are legally documented. Tough conversations are necessary, as they ensure that your intentions for your legacy are understood and respected.

**Suggested Topics For Tough Conversations**

- Do you have life insurance?
- Do you have LTC Insurance? (Long Term Care)
- Where is the insurance policy kept?
- Do you want to be an organ donor?
- Do you want to be cremated or do you want to be buried?
- Who do you want to have access to your passwords & bank accounts?
- Do you want to be buried or placed in a mausoleum?
- Do you have a living will?
- Do you want a funeral?
- Do you want to be resuscitated?
- Do you have a medical and financial POA? (Power of Attorney)
- Do you have an end-of-life plan? (Music, eulogist, clothing, etc.)
- Do you have cash in the house hidden in a secret place?
- Do you have a safe in the house? If so, what is the combination or where do you store the key?
- Do you have a safety deposit box at a financial institution?
- Who will receive certain assets, like family heirlooms and jewelry?

**For business owners...**

- What is going to happen with your business?
- Does it end with you?
- Do you want the business to close?
- Who is your successor?
- Am I Running Out of Time?

***"So, teach us to number our days, that we may apply our hearts unto wisdom." (Psalm 90:12)***

Many people believe that they are too old to begin to think about legacy. They feel like they are running out of time. Let me dismantle that fear. If you feel like you are running out of time or you don't believe you have enough time, do not worry and decide to do nothing. Make the most of whatever time you think you have left. This approach removes the excuse of not having enough time. It is important to remember that it's not the quantity of time you have left, it's the quality of that time that you have left.

Jesus had the greatest impact on the world despite not having a long life. He was only on earth for 33 years, but the quality of the time He spent here depicted the impact He made. Similarly, when you feel like you are running out of time, it is your responsibility to maximize the value of the time you have remaining.

So, how do you maximize the time you believe you have left? There is an old saying, *"You are only as good as your last win."* A critical first step, especially if you feel your time is running short, is to get your legal affairs in order. The state of your legal preparations often speaks volumes about the legacy you leave behind. You may not have always used your time effectively, but once you realize time is limited, the actions you take can compensate for past inactions.

## Legacy Matters Key #117

***God operates beyond the constraints of time.***

He operates from the space of eternity. As believers, we spend our entire lives preparing for eternity. We prioritize eternity over the temporal bounds of time. Why let time distract you from preparing for eternity? Here is the key. While many think of preparing for eternity primarily as preparing for an eternal life in heaven, our preparation goes beyond just reaching heaven. We prepare for eternity by focusing on the impact of our actions in this life and our legacy within our limited time on earth.

What we do during our time on earth echoes into eternity. Therefore, preparing for eternity is not solely about securing a place in heaven. Our preparation for eternity is about what we do in the space of time here on earth and how our actions will resonate eternally. If you feel like you are running out of time, remember that your actions have lasting impacts. What you do in the space of time lives for eternity.

As long as you are breathing, you still have time. Even someone on their deathbed can make impactful decisions, provided they are conscious and capable of doing so. Often, people in such situations are asked to make urgent decisions about important matters. The only time that time really becomes critical is when you no longer have the mental capacity to make decisions. Otherwise, time does not constrain your ability to influence your destiny and shape your legacy. Even when death is knocking at your door, if you are mentally alert and clear in your thinking, you still have time. Feeling like you are running out of time actually indicates that you still have time left, which should prompt you to take action on things you have not done or have done very little.

If you feel that you are running out of time and respond by actively working to rectify certain matters, time might just extend for you as a demonstration of God's love. This is exemplified in the story of Hezekiah (Isaiah 38). The prophet told Hezekiah that his time was up, but Hezekiah was not ready to accept that prophecy. Hezekiah reminded God of his faithfulness. Moved by Hezekiah's plea and actions, God granted him an additional 15 years of life. Even when it seems like time has run out, God can extend time for the sake of fulfilling a greater purpose.

## Legacy Matters Key #118

***Even when it seems like time has run out, God can extend time for the sake of fulfilling a greater purpose.***

Be intentional about every day. Each day is a precious gift. Recognizing this, it is essential to use wisdom and understand that our days are numbered. What do you do in the days that you have been given? Make wise choices and live each day purposefully. In a nutshell, leaders lead. If you are going to build a strong legacy, someone has to take the lead. If you only live from the present, you will not build your legacy. Someone has to take the bull by the horns and be the leader that navigates the tough conversations. You have to be the leader of your own destiny.

# CHAPTER ELEVEN:
# FUTURE MATTERS

***"Before I formed thee in the belly I knew thee; and before thou camest forth out of the womb I sanctified thee, and I ordained thee a prophet unto the nations." (Jeremiah 1:5)***

**Future Forward**

Before you were formed in your mother's womb, God already had a plan for your life. Your purpose was already solidified within you. Your destiny was already set. Your creation was intentionally predicated upon the future. Everything God does is influenced by and speaks from the future.

God operates and communicates from a perspective beyond our present time. His actions and words originate from the future, emphasizing the significance of what is to come. God interacts with us and shapes our existence from a forward-looking viewpoint. He does not address us in our current circumstances but speaks to us from the space of our future.

## Legacy Matters Key #119

***In order to build a strong legacy, you have to see your future in the present moment.***

In Genesis 12:2, God does not address Abraham based on his current situation but rather communicates with him about his destiny and what has already been set in place for him. *"And I will make of thee a great nation, and I will bless thee, and make thy name great; and thou shalt be a blessing."* God speaks to Abraham from Abraham's future. In order to build a strong legacy, you have to see your future in the present moment. You have to see and embrace your future now and lead your life based on that future vision while you are in the present.

Your future matters when it comes to legacy. If you want to intentionally build a strong legacy, you must live from the future with the understanding that your future is now. Once you understand that the future is an extension of your current actions, you will start making decisions that reflect the significance of the future. Many people lack this perspective. They live each day based on what is happening in the present. Their immediate circumstances dictate their daily life.

Have you ever heard anyone say, *"I can't do anything about what's going to happen in the future?"* Well, yes you can. You have the power to influence your future outcomes. God knows the end from the beginning (Isaiah 46:10). Why? Because your future matters. Recognizing the importance of the future shapes your thinking and actions according to your vision of what is to come. The challenge for many people is they live their lives reacting to the present rather than proactively shaping their future.

## Legacy Matters Key #120

***Everything God does is guided by a vision of the future.***

Most people unknowingly live from the future, but they do not grasp the gravity of how their decisions in the present affect their future. For example, some people work two full weeks before receiving payment. That is living from the future. They work for two weeks with the expectation that they will be paid on a future date. Their decisions during those two weeks are based on the assumption that their employer will fulfill their promise to pay them. We often apply this future-oriented thinking in subtle ways in our daily lives, but many of us fail to extend it to more significant areas of our lives, and for the things that matter the most.

***"For I know the plans I have for you, declares the LORD, plans for welfare and not for evil, to give you a future and a hope." (Jeremiah 29:11, ESV)***

Everything God does is guided by a vision of the future. Everything God created, He created with the finished thought in mind. Similarly, that is the way God created us to think and believe. The guidance I am offering you is focused on your future because that is how God communicates with us. He never speaks to us in the present tense. When God speaks to you, His words come from a future perspective because He knows the end from the beginning.

The task for the believer is to see your future as God sees it. So, what is your future? The future is not defined by material possessions or wealth. The future is living a life that aligns with God's values and fulfilling the goals He has set for you. When God says, *"I know the plans I have for you,"* it implies that to comprehend our future, we must understand God's thoughts and intentions for us. God's word depicts His thoughts and intentions for us, which is clearly stated in John 10:10, *"I am come that they might have life, and that they might have it more abundantly."* (John 10:10)

God clearly reveals to us what our future holds in John 10:10. Unfortunately, many believers die without ever realizing the life God intended for them because they were too focused on their past or their present conditions. However, God is not speaking to us about our past or present. He speaks from His plans and visions for our future. God's voice is not predicated upon your past or present circumstances. It is predicated upon how He sees your future.

## Legacy Matters Key #121

***When God speaks concerning your future, you have the responsibility and the grace to embrace it and walk in it.***

This is where the grace of God comes into play. Your past and present circumstances do not matter. When you hear God speaking to you concerning a thing, you don't have to qualify for it, other people do not need to qualify you for it. You do not need to earn or justify it. God has already designated it as your future. When God speaks concerning your future, you have the responsibility and the grace to embrace it and walk in it. It is your responsibility to act on it, embody it, and get a revelation of it. This is where many fall short and find themselves living beneath their God-given privilege.

***(As it is written, I have made thee a father of many nations,) before him whom he believed, even God, who quickeneth the dead, and calleth those things which be not as though they were. 18 Who against hope believed in hope, that he might become the father of many nations, according to that which was spoken, So shall thy seed be. 19 And being not weak in faith, he considered not his own body now dead, when he was about an hundred years old, neither yet the deadness of Sarah's womb: 20 He staggered not at the promise of God through unbelief; but was strong in faith, giving glory to God; 21 And being***

***fully persuaded that, what he had promised, he was able also to perform. (Romans 4:17-21)***

God tells Abraham, *"I'm going to make you a father of many nations."* However, simply declaring this does not make Abraham the father of many nations. According to Romans 4:18, Abraham's belief in God's promise is what makes him a father of many nations. Abraham had to live from the future. It didn't happen because God said it was going to happen. The key moment involves Abraham's faith, as described in Romans 4:18. Abraham believed despite his past and present circumstances, *"Who against hope believed in hope, that he might become the father of many nations, according to that which was spoken."*

Despite having no reason to hope and despite his current circumstances, Abraham chose to believe in the possibility of what God had promised. The phrase "who against hope, believed in hope" illustrates Abraham's decision to trust in God's word, believing that he could become the father of many nations just as God had promised. This does not necessarily align with what Abraham sees as his current or potential reality. Yet, the Bible emphasizes that Abraham's faith was paramount in God's promise being fulfilled in his life. God had declared Abraham to be the father of many nations, but Abraham still needed to actively believe and embrace his destiny.

## Legacy Matters Key #122

***Your future energizes your present actions and decisions.***

In Romans 4:19, Abraham's strong faith is further highlighted. Despite being about a hundred years old and facing the physical limitations of his age and Sarah's inability to conceive, Abraham refused to dwell on his present circumstances and those things that appeared to contradict what God had spoken to him. Instead, he focused on God's promise, not allowing doubt to weaken his faith. *"And being not weak in faith, he considered not his own body now dead, when he was about a hundred years old, neither yet the deadness of Sarah's womb."* (Romans 4:19)

Verses 20 and 21 further illustrate his unwavering belief. Abraham did not doubt God's promise. He remained steadfast in faith, giving glory to God. Abraham was fully convinced that whatever God promised, He was capable of fulfilling. Abraham's ability to trust in God's promise without faltering is what defines his future. What God declares about your future is key because He speaks from a future perspective, not constrained by your past or present, which ultimately shapes how you live in your present. Your future energizes your present actions and decisions.

Think about it. Like my example in the beginning of this chapter, many people live life from the future, but they may not be aware. How many times have you been in the process of eating breakfast, thinking about what you are going to eat for dinner? The challenge for many people is they don't think far enough into the future. Some only plan as far ahead as the next day or the next meal. However, successful people and those who want to create legacy, plan years ahead - thinking as far ahead as 12 months, three years, five years, or even a lifetime. This approach to life requires a vision and is not for the faint of heart.

Your future is connected to your beginning. You were created from the future with a future-oriented purpose. Think about it, as believers we want to make heaven our home. Well, we originated from the place we aspire to return. The moment you stop trying to live from day-to-day, week-to-week, and month-to-month, and begin to understand what God has planned for your future, your life will take on new meaning and power. Often, we hear people say they can't think about next year because they are just trying to get through each day or each week. They pay their bills and live month-to-month because that is as far as they can go into the future.

## Legacy Matters Key #123

***The mindset of "just getting by" is a cycle perpetuated by making decisions that only address your immediate needs.***

This mindset keeps you in a constant struggle, limiting your capacity to create a strong legacy. However, if you go into the future and begin to see the bigger picture - a year from now, five years from now - your decisions and your decision making will change.

Where do you plan to be a year from now? What will be different in your life at the end of this year, in comparison to last year? Look at the bigger picture. That's future. This future-forward perspective is often neglected.

Many people struggle to think beyond the immediate future. Change starts when you get a vision for the future and then begin to make sacrifices now that you might not have considered before. This is the essence of building legacy. As your decisions gradually reflect your vision, your life will begin to transform. God only shows us part of the vision because seeing the fullness of the big picture might be too overwhelming.

**Do You See What I See?**

***"The only thing worse than being blind is having sight but no vision."***

***~Helen Keller***

In the context of legacy, vision is defined as "the ability to think about or plan the future with imagination or wisdom." Many people wander aimlessly in life. They have physical sight, but they have no vision. If you find that you are not reaching the goals and the aspirations that you set for yourself, it be could that you have sight but no real vision.

In my over 30 years of experience as a pastor and entrepreneur, I have found it particularly challenging to help people to see what I see. God has given everyone the ability to see what others cannot see. Just because others might not see what you see, doesn't mean that your vision isn't real. Let's look at the creation story in the book of Genesis. It is fascinating to consider how God uses the earth as a canvas to manifest His vision. Genesis 1 describes God simply declaring, *"Let there be"* and whatever He spoke into existence came to be. God didn't have to consult anyone. He didn't have to seek the counsel of other people to determine what he was going to speak. He understood that what he saw should BE. He was confident in His vision.

# Legacy Matters Key #124

***The dreams that God has deposited within you are too vast to accomplish single-handedly.***

Be selective with whom you share your dreams and ambitions because you will discover that everyone is not happy for you when you begin to share what God has placed within you. Do not expect everyone to support your vision or rejoice in your success. When God gives you a vision, oftentimes it is bigger than what you can do alone. The dreams that God has deposited within you are too vast to accomplish single-handedly. In fact, if it appears to be something you can achieve by yourself, it likely does not match the bigness of what God envisioned for your life. Everything that God does is on a grand scale.

Right now, you may be wrestling with what God intends for you to do and achieve in your life. You may be facing unprecedented challenges in this particular season. It might be surprising to find that people are not as sympathetic or understanding during these times, especially when you are committed to pursuing what God has placed on the inside of you. Oftentimes, others may not recognize or understand your vision.

From my experience, when you begin to embrace what I call "God-size" visions, it can lead to misunderstandings. People may talk about you and call you crazy. Sometimes you might even question your own mental state. But this is what I refer to as "crazy faith." Sometimes you simply need to have crazy faith if you want to bring to fruition the vision God has shown to you. When I say step out on crazy faith, I am talking about venturing into uncharted territory. You may be the only one in your family or community to take such a path.

## Legacy Matters Key #125

***Just because it has not been done, does not mean that it can't be done.***

Imagine a woman being called to become a firefighter, a profession not commonly pursued by women. Despite its unpopularity and the scarcity of women in the field, she heard God's call and responded. Her family might think she is out of her mind. They may even question her reasons for choosing that path. Yet she chooses to do what she sees. There is something deep within all of us that urges us to pursue our calling. Nothing can satisfy that urge except responding to it.

Your determination to pursue your calling and fulfill your purpose is an indication that there is greatness within you that must be passed on to your children, grandchildren, great grandchildren and generations beyond. It is called legacy. Your leadership depends on its full manifestation.

God has instilled in you a unique business idea or concept, something that you have never seen done before. Just because it has not been done, does not mean that it can't be done. Step out on crazy faith and do it. There are many things we now see in existence that were once not part of the physical world. They only existed in the spiritual realm or within the mind of someone. As believers, we have the duty to manifest these spiritual visions into our physical reality. God has placed within you the ability to bring heaven to earth. This is not just a privilege; it is your responsibility to transform heavenly visions into earthly realities. You must continually ask the question within you and to your family members and community, "Do you see what I see?"

***"And the LORD answered me, and said, Write the vision, and make it plain upon tables, that he may run that readeth it. [3] For the vision is yet for an appointed time, but at the end it shall speak, and not lie: though it tarry, wait for it; because it will surely come, it will not tarry." (Habakkuk 2:2-3)***

When you receive a vision from God, write it down and make the vision plain, clear and understandable, because many people will not be able to see what you see. This is where we often fall short. Many are losing the battle because they refuse to do what God has instructed them to do. If you are not careful, you can become so familiar with God that you take Him for granted and fail to do what He called you to do. Remember, God is the same yesterday, today and forever. God remains constant, unchanging through time, but you and I change and evolve. Therefore, God is always at work, renewing and updating.

## Legacy Matters Key #126

***Vision is a journey that begins with discovery.***

Everyone may not resonate with what God has placed in your heart, but that does not invalidate your vision. It is important to be excited about your vision, even if no one else shares your enthusiasm. You must champion your own cause. Shout about it if necessary. After all, you cannot expect others to be excited about something if you are not visibly passionate about it yourself. You have to rehearse it over and over again in your mind until what you rehearse becomes your reality.

Vision is a journey that begins with discovery. Once you discover your vision, you must desire it. Once you desire it, you have to make a decisive commitment to it, learning to articulate your vision clearly. Then you have to learn to dream about its possibilities. However, dreaming alone isn't enough; you must also declare your vision aloud, sharing what you saw and when you saw it. Do not allow anyone to undermine your confidence or deter you from your path. Do not allow anyone to cause you to run away from what God has shown you. Stand firm against any discouragement as you pursue what God has revealed to you.

This is how you stand in your leadership, leading yourself and then creating the path for others to follow. This is how you live from the future and build a strong legacy. I declare that now is the time for you to step into what God has planned for you. But remember, documenting your vision is essential because it helps you outline the steps necessary to achieve what God has intended for your life.

**Education Matters**

Leaving a strong legacy for your children's children requires education. Education matters when it comes to legacy.

**Allow me to share a bit more of my story…**

*My wife and I founded and operated a comprehensive learning center for 20 years. One of the driving forces behind the learning center was our belief in the importance of education. Education matters. We dedicated ourselves to teaching and empowering students from infancy through college. Building on this foundation we established our college of theology, which is now an accredited college.*

*Education is a fundamental tool for building a lasting legacy. By initiating education from infancy and extending it to higher education, we aimed to create a continuum of learning that would equip children with the knowledge, skills, and values needed to impact their communities positively. This approach not only helps in shaping well-rounded individuals but also instills in them a sense of responsibility and a vision for the future. Our goal was to foster environments where students could grow intellectually, emotionally, and spiritually. The establishment of an accredited college as part of this educational pathway allows us to further solidify this legacy, ensuring that students are not only well-prepared academically but also have a sense of ethical leadership and commitment to making society better.*

*The comprehensive learning center and the college serve as pillars of a lasting educational legacy aiming to transform students into leaders who are capable of creating positive changes in their communities. Our future forward vision is for our legacy of education to continue across generations, fostering a cycle of learning that upholds our foundational values and vision.*

I have always believed that education is important, but it was not until a conversation with my accountant that I began to appreciate its value from a different perspective. He shared that although his parents had limited means, they were very intentional about providing the best educational opportunities they could for their children. Although his parents had very little, somehow they were able to put him and his siblings in the best position educationally that they could. His parents' story always stood out to him. His parents' dedication made a lasting impression on him and influenced how he approached educating his children. As a result, he sent his children to private school.

## Legacy Matters Key #127

***Legacy is created by the actions we take during our lives, not just the memories we leave behind.***

Growing up, I attended public school and received a good education. The rigor was different then. When I first had my children, I did not see the value in investing in private schools for my children, despite having the means to do so. However, after hearing my accountant's story and the concept of building a lasting legacy through education, my wife and I decided to enroll our children in private school. They attended private and boarding schools for the duration of their education. We have continued this commitment with my grandchildren.

Again, legacy is not about what happens when you die. My wife and I gave our children and grandchildren the gift of education while we were living. Our decision is not just about offering them a better education. It is about giving them a lasting legacy that no one can take away. It's a gift I've chosen to give while I am still here, reinforcing that a legacy is created by the actions we take during our lives, not just the memories we leave behind.

My children will always be able to say, *"My parents gave us the gift of education because of their love for us."* Love always seeks to give the advantage. So, if love always seeks to give the advantage, then my responsibility is to give to those that I love the best that I can give. Yes, it was challenging. Yes, there were times that I felt like I could be doing something else with the money. But at the end of the day, God allowed us to do it and our family is better because of it.

My daughter could not afford to send my granddaughter to private school. Just as she and I were having that conversation, I remembered that conversation with my accountant. I also remember Dr. Leroy Thompson, a successful pastor and entrepreneur, talking about the importance of investing in his grandchildren's future. These reflections reinforced my belief in positioning the next generation for success, ensuring they can continue the family legacy. At the end of the day, you want to make sure that your children and grandchildren have been positioned to carry on the legacy.

## Legacy Matters Key #128

***Education is the cornerstone of legacy and leadership.***

It gives me great joy to be able to support my grandchildren's education, just as we did with my own children. Education does matter. It is a cornerstone of legacy and leadership. It gives your children an advantage. If you do not see that investment as a significant part of building a lasting legacy, then all you will see is a financial burden. It is also important for your children to recognize this investment as a gift, especially in families where such education is expected and taken for granted. My children might think, well, that is just what Papa does. However, it is essential that they understand that it is more than that. It is a gift. It is about creating a living legacy for them.

Each time I pay my grandchildren's tuition, I am reminded of this commitment, and I am grateful for the opportunity. I am grateful to be able to see the fruit of my labor. This act of support is my way of shaping a living legacy for my family, just as I have with my children. That is the true value of our investment.

Financial literacy is also very important for your children and family. Discussing how you achieved certain milestones, like buying a house or a car, and the significance of managing money is essential. I constantly talk to my children about these topics, and they see me practicing what I preach. However, the key challenge is ensuring that they not only hear your words but also see you living out those principles. The message must be modeled. It is beneficial for them to see you modeling the behavior you teach. It is not just about what you say. It is also about what they observe in action.

## Legacy Matters Key #129

***Financial literacy is important for your children and family.***

Below are a few sample topics for discussion that my family shares in our family times of sharing. We specifically address financial issues. I believe it is important to tackle these discussions early in their lives. Then I challenge their plans. I let them know that if my questioning frustrates them, it indicates that their plan might not be robust enough, or they really do not have a plan.

| Topic | Description |
|---|---|
| What are your financial goals? | Discuss overall financial objectives. |
| What are your goals for this year? | Outline specific targets for the current year. |
| Where do you want to be by this time next year? | Set expectations for your financial position one year from now. |
| What is your plan to get there? | Detail the steps and strategies to achieve your defined goals. |
| **REMINDER** | If questioning the plan causes frustration, it may indicate that the plan is not robust, or you don't have a real plan. Go back and think about it. |

# CHAPTER TWELVE:
# LEGAL MATTERS

***"Even so faith, if it hath not works, is dead..." (James 2:17)***

**Plan or Pain – You Choose**

Legacy is multidimensional. Many people associate legacy with tangible items left behind, such as money, houses, and the level of fame one achieved, the things that can be touched and felt. These elements certainly contribute to one's legacy and are the things that people will observe after you die. However, legacy also encompasses intangible elements like family values, work ethic and family traditions.

As a pastor, I have cultivated a deep respect and love for God within my family that I hope will be passed down through generations. Additionally, I have imparted values such as entrepreneurship, wealth creation, and a strong work ethic to my children and grandchildren. These values encourage hard work, commitment, and dedication to be voices of change within our communities. The intangible aspects of legacy often hold a more lasting significance within the family.

## Legacy Matters Key #130

***People often remember you by your final actions or inactions.***

As I continue to raise my children and grandchildren, these values are likely to be passed on to the next generations. My prayer is that they recognize my influence, just as I've acknowledged my parents and ancestors throughout this book. This cycle of teaching/mentoring and learning is perhaps the most lasting part of legacy, especially those who may not have significant tangible assets to leave behind.

In considering the various dimensions of legacy, there are key planning strategies to consider to ensure your desired legacy is firmly established and preserved. Regardless of what you achieve in life, creating a plan is paramount. People often remember you by your final actions or inactions. The first step is to secure a knowledgeable tax and estate planning attorney as soon as possible. Your tax and estate planning attorney will help you facilitate the process with ease.

I have an excellent tax and estate planning attorney who conveyed the importance and urgency of estate planning before a health crisis potentially occurs in your life. He encounters many of his clients in probate cases who deeply miss their deceased parents and wish they could have more time with them. However, many desire the additional time wishing they could have avoided the complex legal processes that arise when someone fails to properly plan for their transition. Without clear directives, families can face significant turmoil upon the death of a loved one, often having to rely on state laws or ambiguous personal recollections about their loved one's wishes. This lack of clarity often exacerbates the pain of loss.

## Legacy Matters Key #131

***Family conflicts can be avoided by providing clear, written instructions regarding your final wishes.***

Families go through enough anxiety and sadness when their loved one dies. If their loved one was in pain while they were alive, the family is happy they are no longer in pain. They often comfort themselves by saying, "They are in a better place," but the process of determining the distribution of their belongings and assets adds to the pain of the loss.

Family conflicts can be avoided by providing clear, written instructions regarding your final wishes. The details should be legally documented while you are alive so that your family has a clear understanding of your preferences. For instance, if Mom had one wedding ring but two daughters, and after her death, one of the daughters decides to take the wedding ring for herself, it can cause a major upset between the siblings and possibly the whole family. Prior planning, specifying which daughter should receive the ring could prevent potential family drama and pain. Simple, explicit directives can keep familial bonds intact and prevent long-lasting disputes among loved ones.

Based on my personal experience and numerous conversations with my tax and estate attorney, the following information will assist you in beginning the process of estate planning for you and your loved ones. The greatest challenge for those who neglect estate planning are the numerous legal and practical issues that the family encounters after their loved one dies. These issues often complicate the process for the family.

Many people do not realize that they already have an estate plan, one that the state provides by default. Whether you realize it or not, you are covered by a state-devised plan. The question is, does the state's plan suit your needs? If the state's plan does not suit your needs, you have the option to opt out and create your own tailored plan. The key in this process is not just having a plan, but having a well thought out plan. Some people choose to rush the process, turning to services like LegalZoom or other services that offer generic, cookie cutter solutions. These predefined options can be limiting because you can only select what they have to offer.

It is like going into the store to purchase a bag of Lay's potato chips. If you don't like salt on your potato chips, then you probably will not purchase Lay's because they don't come that way. The options for Lay's chips are salted. There are no other options in that category. Unsalted chips are not an option. If you were to make your own chips, then you can customize your version exactly the way you like them.

## Legacy Matters Key #132

***Estate planning is vital.***

In the same way, creating your own estate plan allows for personalization to address your specific circumstances. Estate planning is vital. It can even be exciting when you recognize its potential to address specific family circumstances. Many people have the misconception that estate planning is solely about passing on significant wealth accumulated over a lifetime. However, that is a narrow view of estate planning.

What if you did not accumulate significant wealth over your lifetime? If you have an adult child with substance abuse issues, or family members who struggle with money management issues, you can make strategic plans to deal with these challenges. If you have a special needs child who receives government benefits, estate planning is vital to ensure that any inheritance you may have does not disqualify them from these benefits. Estate planning is not just about who inherits your assets. It is about creating a plan tailored to your family's unique needs and concerns.

An important aspect of estate planning is incapacity planning, which mainly focuses on the management and distribution of assets. It also includes preparing for times when you might be unable to make decisions for yourself. This could involve needing assistance from family members to manage financial obligations, like paying your bills, or helping you make medical decisions before you die. Incapacity planning can be more important than the documents dealing with death, because while we each die only once, incapacity can occur multiple times throughout our lives. It may require others to step in repeatedly to manage your affairs and communicate with medical professionals on your behalf.

## Legacy Matters Key #133

***An important aspect of estate planning is incapacity planning, which mainly focuses on the management and disposition of assets.***

When should you start the process of estate planning? You can begin estate planning as soon as you send your child off to college. Usually, a child is around the age of 18 when they leave home, or they will be turning 18 shortly thereafter. Once children reach the age of 18, they gain legal control over their personal and medical information. Due to HIPPA regulations, parents can no longer access their child's information without their child's consent. In times past, parents could easily inquire about their child's health and receive information from their child's doctors. However, today, once a child turns 18 years of age, this changes. Due to privacy laws, doctors are no longer obligated to share the patient's health information with parents unless they have written permission.

To address this and to avoid complications, families can proactively arrange for a healthcare power of attorney. If their child falls ill while away at college due to meningitis, the flu, COVID, or another illness, the parents can legally make the necessary medical decisions. This legal document allows their child to appoint their parents as their healthcare power of attorney, thereby granting the parents the authority to make medical decisions and receive medical information on their behalf. This not only reduces the emotional stress during such times but also prevents the logistical and financial burden of seeking conservatorship later. This is a practical solution to ensure parents can continue to assist their children with medical needs after they turn 18. This issue is not limited to young adults. Incapacity planning is equally important across all age groups.

On the other end of the spectrum, you may encounter situations where your loved ones experience mental decline, such as dementia or other degenerative conditions that impair their cognitive functions. At this point, many people will seek to arrange for a power of attorney for their loved ones under these circumstances. Their loved one is no longer thinking clearly. They may be suffering from mild dementia or frequent memory lapses. This illustrates the importance of proactive planning, as obtaining legal documents like a power of attorney is complicated once mental decline is significant.

## Legacy Matters Key #134

***Obtaining legal documents like a power of attorney is complicated once mental decline is significant.***

Again, having an incapacity plan established before a diagnosis or before a condition worsens significantly alleviates the family's burden. That way, if your loved one requires care, the person they designated to manage their needs can do so without interference and complications. This proactive approach eliminates the need for stressful and urgent visits to an attorney to figure out how to legally support and care for your loved one's needs.

Far too often, families attempt to address incapacity planning too late, at a point when their loved one no longer has the capacity to legally sign documents or delegate decision-making authority. In such cases, the only recourse is a costly and complex conservatorship proceeding, which often requires hiring multiple attorneys. Preparing these documents in advance can significantly ease the challenges families face not only for financial matters but also for healthcare decisions. Incapacity planning can cover financial management, HIPAA releases, and advanced healthcare directives. These tools significantly ease the burden when unexpected life events occur, providing a structured framework to manage these challenges efficiently. No one likes paying for insurance, but if you are involved in a car accident, you are glad you had it.

As a pastor, it often concerns me when I speak to believers who do not have a more widespread recognition of the need for practical life preparations and estate planning. Attending church and studying the Bible is all about preparing for the next life and naturally align with preparing for the next part of life. The truth is, death is not just a possibility but a certainty, so everyone should prepare for it. By doing so, we can ensure that we pass on our legacy effectively and manage financial and medical matters efficiently.

There have been many cases where the grandparents worked hard to accumulate enough money to purchase a home or a small parcel of land, but unfortunately had no estate planning documents in place. After the grandmother passed away, whomever was residing in the house continued to live there, assuming responsibility for paying the property taxes. However, if something happens to that person and they are unable to continue paying the taxes, the family loses out on the tangible assets that the grandparents left to them. Without an estate plan, there is no clear directive on how to manage or distribute the property. Family members often lack guidance on what steps to take next. Consequently, the tangible legacy that was built with so much effort can be lost to a tax sale. This scenario highlights the importance of having a solid estate plan in order to preserve and pass on assets effectively.

## Legacy Matters Key #135

***Death is not just a possibility but a certainty, so everyone should prepare for it.***

Below is a summary of some of the legal documents you should have in place.

**i. DEATH DOCUMENTS**

Death documents typically take the form of either a will or a trust.

**WILLS.** A will is a letter to the court. Essentially, it tells the Probate Court judge, "This is my last will and testament. The person named here is my executor, and I have chosen them to administer my estate in a specific manner." A will details all the instructions regarding who receives what, when, and how. The role of the court is then to oversee the administration of the estate. Having a will means that the estate must go through probate. A will essentially serves as a formal communication to the court.

In some states, wills must be witnessed. For example, in the state of Tennessee, wills must be witnessed, adhering to a specific legal process to ensure that the documents are valid under law. The key requirement is that the will must be signed in the presence of the witnesses, both sight and sound. This means that the person executing the will must be in the same room as the witnesses during the signing process. This method of witnessing has been standard for hundreds of years. Observing these formalities ensures the document is legally valid. Failure to follow these procedures can render even the best-prepared will invalid. For example, if a will is signed with only one witness present, and then taken to another room where another witness signs it, the will would be considered invalid. Once the documents are properly executed, then your intentions are securely established.

**TRUSTS.** On the other end of the spectrum, for those who prefer not to subject their family to the probate process, setting up a trust is an alternative. A trust is essentially an agreement between the grantor (the person who creates the trust), and the trustee (the person who is responsible for managing the trust). The trustee's role is to execute the trust's terms for the benefit of the beneficiaries. This creates a three-party agreement where the grantor and the trustee enter into a contract to benefit a third party, the beneficiary. In this setup, the grantor transfers property and instructions to the trustee, who then administers these assets for the beneficiaries.

The trustee holds legal title to the property as defined in the trust, which effectively gives them control over the property according to the specific instructions within the trust document. For instance, if the grantor instructs the trustee to distribute funds to their children at ages 25, 27, and 30, the trustee is obligated to follow these instructions. If one of the children requests funds at age 21, the trustee is under fiduciary obligation to adhere to the terms of the trust as they are specified, not based on personal discretion. In this case, the trustee would need to deny the request, explaining that the trust does not permit any distributions until the age of 25, as explicitly directed by the grantor.

Trusts typically end up in court when the trustee breaches the terms in a significant way. For example, if a trust stipulates that a beneficiary is to receive $100 a month starting at age 21, and the beneficiary has not received any payments, this could prompt legal action. The beneficiary recognizing the discrepancy and being competent and of age, has the right to approach the court for resolution. In such cases, the court is likely to remove the trustee for failing to execute the grantor's explicit instructions.

Creating a trust allows the property to bypass the probate process. Essentially, the trust acts as a directive from the grantor to the trustee. As long as the trustee complies with the instructions laid out in the trust agreement, the administration of the trust typically does not require court intervention. Choosing the right trustee is important to ensure the trust is followed as intended and to keep family matters out of court. If the trustee can faithfully execute the terms laid out by the grantor, a trust can effectively prevent legal disputes. This makes it an essential option to consider when deciding how to manage your estate.

**ii. Incapacity Planning**

**Financial Power of Attorney.** Incapacity planning often involves setting up a financial power of attorney. The financial power of attorney is a legal identity assignment. Essentially, when you grant someone financial power of attorney, it allows them to act on your behalf in financial matters. This means they can walk into your bank and perform any transaction or exercise any right as though they were you. When appointing someone as financial power of attorney, you must choose wisely. Focus on the role rather than your relationship with the person.

Ideally, the person entrusted with this responsibility should be financially responsible and not someone who frequently borrows money from you. If they have a habit of borrowing, they may be tempted to use your resources if you become incapacitated, since they control the purse strings. While such actions for personal gain could lead to legal consequences, often the most stringent outcome is a court judgment against the agent, which essentially results in an IOU to the principal. Therefore, selecting the right person for this role from the start is essential to avoid potential misuse of authority and legal complications.

By setting up a financial power of attorney you are safeguarding the assets you have acquired. Should you become disabled or incapacitated, you have designated someone who can manage your financial affairs just as you would if you were able. The appointed person will be able to continue handling your financial responsibilities in your stead.

You have the option of granting a general power of attorney, which allows the appointed person to handle all aspects of your affairs, or a limited power of attorney, which restricts them to specific actions you designate. For example, if your family has professionals like an attorney, a real estate expert, and an accountant, you might assign each person a limited power of attorney tailored to their expertise, allowing them to effectively manage specific areas of your affairs. This approach is like assembling a team where each member contributes their unique skills.

Additionally, you can decide when the power of attorney becomes active. There are two types: 1) springing, which only takes effect under certain conditions, such as the principal's incapacitation; and 2) immediate, which becomes effective as soon as it is executed.

My attorney typically recommends immediate powers of attorney, as springing powers of attorney sometimes requires a physician's certification to confirm the person is in fact disabled before they become effective. A springing power of attorney is suitable if you have family members or friends you want to empower to act on your behalf but do not fully trust them to do so without a verified medical opinion confirming your inability to manage your affairs.

The financial power of attorney is essential for protecting your assets and ensuring that your business and financial matters can continue smoothly without interrupting the flow of money to your family, even if you become sick or incapacitated. It ensures that your personal health issues do not interrupt the financial operations or the flow of commerce within your family.

**Healthcare Power of Attorney.** The healthcare power of attorney functions similarly but in the medical decision-making context. When you establish a healthcare power of attorney, you are preparing for a situation where you might become incapacitated, and someone needs to discuss your medical treatment with your physician. Again, think about the role, not just the relationship. If you have a close relationship with someone who rarely contacts you and with whom you have never discussed medical issues, they may not be the best choice for your healthcare power of attorney. Instead, it would be better to choose someone who communicates with you regularly, is easy to talk to about medical issues, and whom you trust to keep your medical information confidential.

Medical details can be sensitive and not all information is something you might want widely shared. Remember, most powers of attorney do not include a non-disclosure agreement. So, the person you appoint will have access to all your medical records just as you would, as it is a legal identity assignment. Therefore, it is essential to select someone who will respect your privacy because they will legally be able to obtain any medical information you can access. This choice is not just about managing your health decisions. It is also about protecting your privacy. Choose wisely to ensure that the person holding your healthcare power of attorney respects and honors your information.

**Living Wills.** People often confuse wills and living wills due to similar terminology, but they serve very different purposes. A will is a document that specifies how one's assets should be distributed after death. In contrast, a living will is used to communicate a person's preferences for medical treatment in the event they become terminally ill. This document only becomes effective in those circumstances. The living will is only operative if the condition is terminal.

For instance, if someone is treated for a condition like brain cancer and is given a limited time to live, a living will would then guide medical decisions. This ensures that their treatment preferences are respected, relieving family members from making painful and potentially divisive decisions about end-of-life care.

Consider a scenario where a doctor informs the family that nothing more can be done medically for their loved one who is nearing the end of life. If that person then stops breathing, a living will prevents medical staff from using extraordinary measures like a respirator, avoiding a situation where the family is burdened with making critical medical decisions in a moment of crisis. A living will clarifies one's wishes regarding life-sustaining treatment, thereby protecting family members from the emotional strain of deciding how a loved one should pass away. The living will allows you to control how you die, allowing you to be able to die with dignity.

**Advanced Healthcare Directive.** An advanced healthcare directive is a two page document that doctors in most states are used to seeing. It is a healthcare power of attorney. It combines elements of a healthcare power of attorney and a living will. A copy of the document is given to the person's attending physicians so that in the event they are admitted to the hospital and unable to communicate, the medical staff will already have the necessary information on file. This includes details about who to contact and who has been designated as their healthcare agents, ensuring that their medical and personal wishes are respected even when they are unable to speak for themselves.

**Pour-over Wills.** A pour-over will is done with trust-based estate plans. This type of will is designed to address any assets that were not already placed in trust by the time of your death. The key provision in a pour-over will states that any assets owned at the time of death which are not already titled in the name of the trustee of the family trust, should be transferred ("poured over") into the family trust and distributed according to the terms of that trust.

The pour-over will simplifies the probate process significantly because it contains just one primary instruction, to transfer all assets into the trust. This instrument is important, especially if the trust was not fully funded during your lifetime. If certain assets were not titled to the trustee, the pour-over will ensures they are included in the trust upon your death. This consolidation of assets under one instruction streamlines the legal process, minimizing the complexities typically associated with probate.

**Finally…**

These are the essential documents involved in comprehensive estate planning, covering the major components needed to manage your assets effectively. The estate planning process can vary from one attorney to another, but generally it begins with the attorney gathering detailed information. This involves not only collecting data about your assets but also understanding your family dynamics and any specific concerns you may have, such as a family member with special needs or substance abuse issues. After all the relevant information is gathered, the attorney will be able to understand the client's desires regarding their incapacity planning and the disposition of their assets. Then he/she can begin to devise the plan for your needs.

Next, the attorney may schedule a design meeting where he/she presents the proposed plan to you. During this meeting, you can ask questions and suggest modifications, such as reallocating assets or addressing new concerns that may have arisen. This interaction is key as it helps refine the plan to ensure it specifically caters to your specific needs and desires. Initially, the plan may seem somewhat standard, but your feedback and additional instructions help move the plan away from a "cookie cutter" model to one that is tailored to your specific situation. Then upon review, the signing ceremony is scheduled where you execute the final documents.

Once the estate plan is fully established, it is essential to maintain and update it regularly. Periodic meetings should be held with your attorney to discuss any changes in your life and family circumstances. This includes assessing whether the individuals named in the estate plan are still appropriate choices for your designated roles and whether any new assets need to be titled to the trust. Once you create an estate plan it should evolve with your life. As changes occur in your life, whether in family dynamics, asset accumulation, or personal preferences, your estate plan needs to be adjusted accordingly. Estate planning is not a one-time transaction. It is an ongoing process that requires continuous attention, similar to financial planning. Your estate plan needs to adapt and change as you move through different phases of life.

**Common Mistakes in Estate Planning**

There are many mistakes that people make in terms of estate planning. Some common legal mistakes people make when planning their estate include failing to update the will, not considering the tax implications of their decisions, neglecting to include digital assets, and overlooking the need for a durable power of attorney or healthcare directive.

One of the most common and significant mistakes in estate planning is simply failing to engage in the process at all. Neglecting estate planning can lead to serious consequences. The estate planning process also involves examining how your assets are titled, reviewing beneficiary designations, and taking other steps to solidify your plans for the future. These steps ensure that your affairs are in order whether you are physically unable to manage your affairs or when you die.

**The Use of DIY Estate Planning Methods.** Many people use do-it-yourself estate planning methods, such as downloading wills from the internet and signing them without proper witnesses or following the required signing procedures. This typically results in the will being invalidated.

Estate planning and tax considerations are closely related. Many estate planning decisions have tax consequences. For example, if a person adds their name to their mother's house deed, it is considered a gift from the mother at that time, valued at half the property's worth on the date of the transfer. This gifting not only affects the mother's tax responsibilities but also transfers certain tax liabilities to the person inheriting the house. This illustrates why it's crucial to approach estate planning with a comprehensive understanding of both legal and tax implications.

**Inheritance Risks for Beneficiaries Receiving Need-Based Government Assistance.** Many people make the mistake of drafting a will that leaves assets to a beneficiary who receives need-based government benefits. Need-based benefits are granted on the condition that the recipient has little to no income or assets. Therefore, inheriting money can disqualify them from continuing to receive these benefits. This situation often arises when someone intends to provide for a loved one with special needs through a will but does not fully understand the implications. They are probably unaware that leaving a substantial sum of money to a beneficiary on need-based government assistance can inadvertently harm them by making them ineligible for their existing benefits.

As a result, the beneficiary may lose their eligibility for the benefits and be forced to rely entirely on the inheritance. Once the inherited funds are depleted, they must reapply for their government benefits. Typically, the process of requalifying for these benefits is lengthy, often three to six months or more, during which they will be without the necessary support. As a result, they may face potential financial hardship while waiting to regain their benefits, a significant unintended consequence of what was meant to be a generous act.

**Delayed Action in Estate Settlement.** When someone passes away leaving you property or they leave a will, do not delay in taking action. Memories fade and documents can be misplaced over time. For example, there was a woman who had been living in a house for 15 years. She had a copy of a will that bequeathed the house to her; however, it was just a copy. While a copy can be used in probate, it can be challenged if anyone contests its validity claiming it doesn't reflect the intentions of the one who passed. The court may then dismiss the copy of the will because it is not the original will.

These complications can be avoided by promptly initiating the probate process and handling property title transfers immediately after the owner dies. By acting quickly, you ensure that all necessary information is still accessible. Conversely, delaying these actions, like in this case for 15 years, sets you up for potential failure and complicates the process considerably.

**Legal Complications of Estate Planning After a Dementia Diagnosis.** Delaying incapacity planning until after receiving a dementia diagnosis may impair one's ability to legally execute documents. If someone attempts to sign powers of attorney or wills while under a dementia diagnosis, it can provide grounds for contesting these documents in court. Family members who feel slighted by the estate plan may challenge the validity of the documents by questioning whether the signer had the necessary legal capacity at the time of signing. Attorneys have strategies to mitigate these risks, especially if the attorney is aware of potential issues.

For example, if a person seems coherent and responsive during consultations, answering questions appropriately and understanding the proceedings, it may appear they are capable of signing the documents.

However, if the attorney is not informed of a dementia diagnosis, it can later lead to complications and legal challenges regarding the authenticity of the consent given at the time of signing.

If the attorney was aware of the dementia diagnosis, they could have taken steps to videotape their conversations with the client. Even with a dementia diagnosis there are periods known as lucid intervals during which a person may fully understand their actions. Videotaping these interactions provides concrete evidence that the client was competent and aware of the implications of their decisions at the time of signing. Without such evidence, relying solely on an attorney's testimony may not be sufficient in court. If the court doubts the attorney's account, it could invalidate the document in question.

**Lack of Estate Planning for Blended Family.** A common and significant oversight occurs when individuals who divorce or remarry fail to update their estate plans, particularly when both parties bring children from previous relationships into the new marriage. This lack of clarity about what happens to their property can lead to complex family disputes.

In blended families where divorce rates are notably high (over 50%), estate planning is very important. Often, both partners bring children from previous relationships into their new marriage, creating a scenario reminiscent of the 1970s sitcom, *The Brady Bunch.* In such cases, the dynamics of inheritance can become complex. For example, if one spouse passes away first, they may leave their entire estate to the surviving spouse. If the surviving spouse is not fond of their stepchildren, they may choose not to pass anything on to them, which can lead to disappointment and family upset.

To address these potential conflicts, blended family estate planning can involve setting up separate trusts. One possible solution is to establish a survivor's trust for the surviving spouse and a family trust for the children. For instance, you might decide to place an apartment building into the family trust, which would then be transferred to your children immediately upon your death. This approach ensures that specific assets are earmarked for your children, protecting their inheritance regardless of the surviving spouse's preferences. In blended family scenarios, estate planning can be meticulously structured to ensure the well-being of both the surviving spouse and any children from previous relationships.

Another example is a person may place the apartment building into a trust managed by a trustee for the benefit of their adult children. They could arrange for the rental income from the apartment complex to go to their surviving spouse for the duration of her life. This setup allows the spouse to benefit from the income, yet ensures that the property itself is preserved for the children's inheritance, regardless of any changes in the spouse's feelings towards them. This is important in blended families to prevent the surviving spouse from potentially disinheriting the deceased's children. It also highlights the importance of reviewing and updating beneficiary designations, especially after remarriage.

People often overlook policies that may still list an ex-spouse as the beneficiary because these details are out of sight and mind, particularly if the policies are managed through automatic payments or are tied to employment. Thorough estate planning ensures that all aspects, including insurance and trusts, are aligned with the current family dynamics and intentions.

**Lack of Communication Around Final Arrangements and Burial Plans.** Another trend since the COVID-19 pandemic in 2020, is an increase in cremations, which historically were not common. Many people choose cremation due to the lower cost, compared to a traditional burial, especially when there is a lack of insurance to cover burial expenses. As a pastor, I have observed that these decisions are frequently made without anything in writing. It is often left to the person managing the estate to declare that the deceased wished to be cremated, despite objections from family members who may have never heard such wishes expressed. This scenario can lead to disputes within families, where the decision to cremate is seen by some as influenced more by financial reasons, either as a cost-saving measure or to avoid financial strain, rather than by the actual wishes of the deceased. This has become a common issue.

Some estate plans include a section dedicated to final arrangements and burial planning. This part of the plan allows you to specify your preferences clearly. The document typically includes options to indicate choices like cremation, no cremation, or to leave the decision entirely to the discretion of the spouse or another designated person. This clarity ensures that your wishes are understood and respected.

You can also specify where you want to be buried, such as a family plot or another significant location. If you have definitive preferences about your final arrangements, such as not wanting to be cremated, you can make these decisions in advance. You can go as far as detailing your attire, the color of the casket, and even selecting who will carry the casket, and secure these plans with a funeral home through a contract. This ensures everyone will follow your instructions precisely to avoid any legal issues, as they will want to honor the agreement made with the person who arranged and paid for the services.

This proactive approach not only reflects changing attitudes but also removes the burden of decision-making from family members. It is important to consider that the cost of a funeral can average around $15,000, making it practical to have an insurance policy that covers these expenses. By planning ahead and possibly purchasing a policy specifically for these costs, you can ensure that your final wishes are carried out without imposing financial stress on your loved ones, allowing them to focus on their emotional well-being during a difficult time.

**Cost of Estate Planning**

The fear of discussing funeral arrangements often stems from concerns about cost. It is important to understand all available options and the benefits of planning ahead to manage and mitigate these costs effectively. My attorney used the analogy of insurance to help me understand the benefits of estate planning. Just as no one enjoys paying for car insurance due to its perceived lack of immediate value, many hesitate to plan for their eventual passing due to associated costs. However, those with insurance can live with peace of mind, knowing they are covered in the event of an accident, without the burden of unexpected expenses. Similarly, estate planning involves upfront costs but can save much greater expenses and distress in the future.

Estate planning offers peace of mind by ensuring that your wishes are known and will be executed as intended, which prevents family disputes and misunderstandings after your passing. The value cannot be easily quantified in monetary terms. Much like insurance, the comfort of knowing you have a plan in place is nearly invaluable. It keeps you from worrying about the potential financial and emotional costs of not being prepared. The most difficult and costly probate cases arise from situations where there was no clear plan, leading to family conflicts. Therefore, investing in a well-organized estate plan is less about the immediate cost and more about securing long-term peace and order for yourself and your loved ones.

In terms of the costs of estate planning, drafting a will or trust typically ranges from $1,200 to $3,500. While some situations require more sophisticated and thus more expensive planning, these figures cover the majority of cases. Most attorneys charge approximately $300 per hour for probate representation. This means that on the lower end, $1,200 would cover approximately four hours of work, while $3,500 would cover about twelve hours. When considering these figures, it is important to compare them to the potential costs of probate if no estate plan is in place.

If you work with experienced attorneys, a seamless estate plan will cost around $3,500, which covers all necessary procedures and ensures compliance with state requirements. This process is comprehensive, generally involving at least 12 hours of work to thoroughly check all legal boxes. If you neglect to plan and your estate goes to probate, you will end up paying at least this amount in legal fees.

If your estate lacks readily accessible funds to cover these costs (say the money is not in the bank and needs to be extracted from assets like your home), this can complicate what you intend to leave to your heirs. For example, if attorney fees and outstanding bills must be settled from estate assets, you might be forced to liquidate something valuable, like a family home that you intended to pass on to your children. Therefore, it is financially wiser to handle these costs upfront rather than leaving them to be dealt with after your passing, which can often lead to unintended consequences for your estate and beneficiaries.

Typically, probate cases without disputes cost between $3,500 and $6,000. However, if there is contention among parties, the fees can escalate significantly. For example, a case that involves intense disagreements costs upwards of $121,000. In comparison, simpler cases where parties are cooperative generally fall within the $70,000 to $80,000 range. Contrast this with the $1,200 to $3,500 that you might spend on an estate plan, which is substantially less costly and provides the added benefit of peace of mind.

**Let's Get Started**

**Legacy Requires Action**

Building a strong legacy requires intentionality. It does not happen with the snap of a finger. You must be intentional about your actions. You must plan. You must educate yourself and your family. You must constantly have the mindset that your life matters right now, in this present moment, and after you leave this life. Remember that YOU matter and that your story, your narrative, your life is worth preserving.

# Legacy Matters Key #136

***Legacy does not happen by chance.***

You have to put in the work. The Bible says in James 2:17, "Faith without works is dead." Faith without corresponding action cannot yield the manifestation of the promises of God in your life. In the same way, your legacy will never outlive you if you don't have intentionality, action, planning, introspection, and an understanding of your value. You have to do the work. Otherwise, everything that you have accomplished, endured, overcome, built and developed will die with you. Doesn't your family deserve better? My answer is, YES! So, here are your first steps. Let's get started right now!

To achieve the greatest results, action is required. The first step is to do something. Do not leave your life and all that you have accomplished and lived in the government's hands. Do not allow their narrative to be your default narrative. Be proactive, particularly when it comes to estate planning. Unlike car insurance, where you may pay premiums for life and may never need to file a claim, estate planning is different. It is based on the unavoidable fact that you will eventually leave this life at some point. There is no getting around it. The fact is everyone will eventually pass away, so planning for the disposition of your assets is an inevitable necessity.

Once you accept this reality, any hesitation, reservation, apprehension, or fear about planning for the future and securing your legacy – including estate planning, purchasing life insurance, health insurance, tough conversations with family that matter, developing and crafting your own story - will dissipate. Many people struggle with acknowledging their mortality and the realization that life in this realm is not forever. Understanding and accepting your mortality can remove much of the fear and hesitation associated with building a strong legacy and significantly ease the apprehension around planning for the future.

# Legacy Matters Key #137

***Designate someone to manage your affairs should you become unable to do so yourself.***

Life is short. The time we spend here on earth is all we have. Therefore, if you want to build and leave a legacy for your family or pass on your possessions in a manner that differs from the default arrangements of your particular state, you must actively engage in estate planning. There are no alternatives. Given that illness often precedes death, I advise you to include incapacity planning in your arrangements. Designate someone to manage your affairs should you become unable to do so yourself.

**Tangible and Intangible Assets – It's All Valuable**

While many people focus on the tangible aspects of their legacy, such as property and money, remember that you can also pass on your values through your estate. If you have accumulated enough of an estate to affect how your loved ones will live after you die, this is a great way to ensure your values are also passed down to them. For example, if you value education, you could stipulate that your children are eligible to an inheritance only if they obtain a college degree. This way you are not only leaving them physical assets but also instilling the importance of education. If you have a child with a substance abuse issue, you could structure your will so that they receive financial distributions only when they achieve certain recovery milestones and report them to the trustee of your estate. This passes on the value of recovery to your family and supports your loved one's journey towards recovery.

Think about your legacy in both tangible and intangible terms. Regardless of your financial situation, whether you have amassed great wealth, live paycheck to paycheck, or face other life challenges, everyone has values that we hope will be upheld by future generations. By strategically using your estate to enforce these values, you ensure that your legacy influences behavior in ways that align with your moral and ethical beliefs. It is not just about what you leave behind, but about why and how you structure those gifts to instill the values you cherish for generations to come.

# Legacy Matters Key #138

***Think about your legacy in both tangible and intangible terms.***

***"And ye shall dispossess the inhabitants of the land, and dwell therein: for I have given you the land to possess it. [54] And ye shall divide the land by lot for an inheritance among your families: and to the more ye shall give the more inheritance, and to the fewer ye shall give the less inheritance: every man's inheritance shall be in the place where his lot falleth; according to the tribes of your fathers ye shall inherit." (Numbers 33:53-54)***

God told the people of Israel that He gave them the land as an inheritance. However, He also makes it clear that to claim this inheritance they had to fight for it. Having to fight for something that is truly yours often makes you value it more. When things come too easily or without conditions, people tend to value them less, sometimes leading to a sense of entitlement and wastefulness. If the inheritance is conditional and the recipients are required to meet certain criteria or make an effort to qualify for it, they tend to value it more.

**Allow me to share this final tidbit of my story…**

*A colleague of mine who was a pastor, passed away and his daughter inherited the church. Upon inheriting the church, his daughter chose to close it because she had no personal investment in keeping it open. If the conditions required her to keep the church open for one year in order to inherit the property, she may have had a different approach. She may have been compelled to find ways to make it work, or otherwise forfeit the property. Maybe she would have transferred the church to another pastor or the congregation, fulfilling her father's wish to keep the church active. Her father's desire was to keep the church open. Estate planning would have given him a strategy that he could have put in place to make that happen.*

After 30 years of pastoring, I have encountered many people grappling with the challenges of their later years. Their struggle is not only about coping with what I term their "seasoned age" but also how they perceive the conclusion of their own stories. It is disheartening to see many fail to enjoy the fruit of their labor, as they contend with declining quality of life in their advanced years. These difficulties often affect what they can pass on to their children and grandchildren.

The challenge many families encounter in deliberately crafting their legacy, and understanding its impact on their family, friends, and community, has profoundly impacted me. This realization has motivated me to help others be more intentional in the process of establishing their legacy. Why? **Love always seeks to give the advantage!**

I firmly believe that everyone leaves a legacy, but the vital question is whether you are leaving the legacy you truly desire. Remember, it is never too late to begin shaping your legacy. Start now, right where you are. You hold the power to author and shape your own story, beginning this very moment. Why? BECAUSE YOU MATTER!

## Legacy Matters Key #139

***Your legacy matters.***

# APPENDIX

***Reflections: Future-Proofing Your Legacy***

Allow me to share a few personal reflections that highlight the importance of future-proofing your legacy…

**Reflection 1**

*One day, I took my 72 year-old mother to her medical appointment. While we were there, I noticed the waiting room was full of senior citizens. I pointed out to my mother the number of elderly people present in the office that day who had driven themselves to their appointments, some using walkers or canes. Many were couples without any assistance from their children. My mother observed that she was the only one there with her son (me) assisting her. It struck me that although we spend most of our lives aiming for retirement, many of us fail to really prepare for it. The new generation does not seem to value caring for their parents as much as my generation was taught, and even my generation sometimes falls short in this regard.*

*As my wife and I consider our future, we wonder who will care for us when we reach the seasoned years of our lives. We realize the importance of ensuring someone is prepared to assist us. We also realize the importance of making preparations for assisted living arrangements, savings, and insurance policies. Many people do not make these preparations, often due to the costs involved. It is very important to think about what happens if you live to an old age or wake up one day without the same strength or health. What will your life and legacy look like then?*

*During the COVID pandemic, my church delivered over 10,000 meals to seniors in various communities. It was heartbreaking to see many of them left to fend for themselves. Loneliness is a significant issue for the elderly, often leading to a decline in their well-being. We spend much of our lives striving to reach seniority and retirement, only to find that it may not be what we expected due to these challenges. Therefore, it is essential to live life to the fullest while we have the strength and vitality to enjoy it.*

**Reflection 2**

*I have a friend, who is also my jeweler. He experienced a sudden medical emergency that changed his life. He was in a coma for five days. When he woke up, he realized he had essentially died and been resuscitated with CPR and heart shocks. This experience gave him a new perspective on life. From Saturday until Monday, he was afraid to sleep, fearing he might die again. Things he previously did not value became incredibly important to him. His daughter was pregnant at the time with his first grandson, and he felt it would have been a tragedy and a travesty if he had died and missed the opportunity to meet his grandson because of the reckless decisions he made concerning his health. He admitted he had ignored his health, refusing to see a doctor despite knowing something was wrong. The whole experience drastically changed his outlook on life.*

*His ex-wife was one of the people who stepped up to take care of him. While I was there visiting him, she asked him a significant question. She said that his daughter wanted to know if he had died, where would he have spent eternity - heaven or hell? She was in tears because they were uncertain. I had the opportunity to lead him to Christ. As I discussed earlier in this book, God is a God of another chance. After leading him to Christ, we Face-Timed his daughter in Texas and shared what had just happened. Both he and his daughter were in tears because he now had another chance, and they no longer had to wonder or guess about his eternal fate.*

*My friend didn't remember anything; he just woke up in the hospital with no memory of what had happened days before. Imagine waking up one day to realize that your life has been altered by an accident, and now you're in the hospital with everything changed.*

*What if you go to the doctor one day and discover you have a life-changing medical condition? These scenarios can dramatically alter your life.*

**Reflection 3**

*Another very good friend of mine also experienced a life-altering event. He was a hardworking, country guy who owned a meat processing company. He built his mom-and-pop business from nothing into a very successful seven-figure enterprise. One day, while working in the processing plant, a chute fell and he reflexively reached out to catch it. To him he felt like he pulled a muscle in his back. For weeks, he tried self-medicating with pain pills, believing he had a minor injury due to catching the chute. However, it turned out to be something more serious. At my urging, he visited my doctor, who discovered he had stage four cancer. The initial injury from the chute had been a blessing in disguise, as it led to this critical diagnosis. The oncologist told him he had a short time to live, and that he had to undergo an aggressive treatment plan.*

*This life-altering event forced him to step away from the business he never thought he could leave, the business from which he thought he could never take vacation, the business he thought was his life. He had to prioritize his health and well-being over work. All he knew was work. However, he was the only one in the family who knew the ins and outs of the family business. He did not have a system in place that allowed for the business to continue without his involvement.*

*But there is good news... Despite being given only six months to live, he is still alive several years later, having come through the treatment with God's help. But from that life-changing situation, everything changed in a moment. This experience completely changed his perspective on life and what he valued. It made me reflect on how quickly life can change and what our legacy will look like in such moments. His story is a testament to how unforeseen events can alter our lives in an instant.*

We all tend to think we have plenty of time. Given my knowledge of various scenarios and having witnessed their impact on families, I realize that I still have work to do in terms of preparation. Being better than average does not equate to being prepared. It simply means you are better off than someone else. We must take it a step further and ensure we have genuinely prepared for any of these possible scenarios. The extent of your preparation is determined by what you want to happen in those situations.

Life happens to all of us. You may feel that you lack the necessary resources to leave the legacy you desire, but not having resources is not an excuse to avoid making preparations. You still have to figure it out. Most people tend to figure things out during a crisis, but don't let crises dictate your way of life. Instead, live life having proactive conversations. Refuse to allow other people's emergencies to become your emergencies. People who live in a constant state of crisis often expect others to drop everything and help. This highlights the importance of thinking through legacy planning.

Many people tend to only address issues when a crisis occurs. However, it is not a matter of if a crisis will occur, but when will a crisis occur. If we are more intentional, especially those with financial challenges, we can make the necessary adjustments. Often, it is about having the determination to get things done. What are the actionable items you can take care of within your power to help facilitate a better outcome? You can still make some preparations even with limited resources.

Now that you have read this life-changing book on legacy matters, I invite you to reflect on the following scenarios. Consider how your life and legacy unfold in these situations. Close your eyes and imagine the following:

## SCENARIO #1

**If you were to die today, where would you spend eternity?**

**Imagine looking down from eternity. What do you see?**

**Does your family know what to do in your absence?**

**What do you see your spouse and family doing based on the preparations you made (or didn't make)?**

**Do they know where to find your insurance policy and other important documents?**

**Are your final wishes clear to them?**

**Is there chaos, confusion, or frustration? Explain in detail.**

**Are there feelings of regret, anger, or resentment? Explain in detail.**

**What are people saying about you now that you are gone?**

## SCENARIO #2

**If you were to experience a life-changing medical emergency, such as a stroke or cancer, what would your life look like?**

**Who would be there to assist you?**

**Do you have the financial resources to maintain your current lifestyle?**

**How would this situation impact your life and legacy?**

**SCENARIO #3**

**What if you were to have a life-altering accident, such as a car accident or a work-related incident that changes your way of life and potentially impacts your legacy. In what ways would your life be different?**

**How would this impact the legacy you leave behind?**

## SCENARIO #4

**Imagine waking up one day and realizing you are 65. You don't have the same job; you can't do the same things; or you are no longer able to work. Despite aiming to reach 65 or what we consider the retirement age, many have not made adequate preparations for it. What preparations have you made for this stage of life?**

**What does life look like for you beyond the age of 65?**

**Are you financially fit for your senior years?**

**Do you have an assisted living policy?**

**Who will handle your primary caregiving needs? If you have any health conditions or issues, who will transport you to and from your medical appointments?**

**FINALLY…**

**Have you considered that one of these four scenarios could be your future? What are your thoughts?**

**How do you envision your family, friends, and relatives reacting?**

**Is this the way you want your story to be told and your legacy to unfold?**

**Does what you see align with your vision for your life?**

**How do you imagine your spouse, family, and relatives responding? Is it the outcome you desire?**

**BE INTENTIONAL...**
**YOUR LEGACY MATTERS!**

# ABOUT THE AUTHOR

Apostle Amos L. Howard, Sr. is a native of Gary, Indiana. He and his wife, Yolanda, are the proud parents of six children, one daughter-in-love, and three grandchildren. Apostle Howard holds a Bachelor of Arts Degree in Psychology/Theology from American Baptist College in Nashville, Tennessee, and a Master of Science Degree in Guidance and Counseling from Tennessee State University.

Apostle Howard's journey of overcoming multi-millions in personal debt fueled his passion to birth Breakthrough Ministries, a teaching platform focused on biblical principles of financial management. His personal experience has shaped his belief that true spiritual freedom cannot be fully realized while under financial bondage. Through his ministry, countless individuals have been liberated from the chains of debt, allowing them to experience both spiritual and financial freedom. To date, Apostle Howard and his ministry have sown tens of thousands of dollars into helping others become debt-free.

His core message revolves around partnership, ownership, stewardship, and discipleship—pillars that reflect his dedication to empowering others to live life abundantly through faith, love, and wise decision-making.

As the Senior Pastor of Living Truth Christian Center in Smyrna, Tennessee, Apostle Howard has faithfully shepherded the congregation for over 30 years, with 39 years of pastoral ministry experience. Under his leadership, the ministry relocated from Monroe Street to its current facility, completing a million-dollar renovation debt-free. Since then, Living Truth has grown exponentially, increasing its assets from $200,000 to millions.

His heart for the community led to the creation of Blessed Beginnings Comprehensive Learning Center, the first African American church daycare in Rutherford County. He further established ALERT Community Development Corporation, a 501(c)(3) initiative focused on education, redevelopment, and training. Through its housing arm, Lazarus House, Living Truth has invested over $1 million to assist families in transitional housing, facilitating homeownership and providing stable living environments for low-to-moderate-income families.

Apostle Howard carries an entrepreneurial anointing and has successfully built a multi-million dollar residential and commercial real estate portfolio. His passion for real estate led to the authorship of "The Earth Is Your Real Estate Property," an essential guide for real estate investors seeking both practical and spiritual foundations for success in the field.

In 2025, Apostle Howard released his latest book, "Legacy Matters: Ensuring Your Legacy Through Intentional Living," a profound work that challenges readers to live "on purpose and in purpose," crafting a legacy that reflects their values, impact, and divine calling. The book serves as a roadmap for personal growth, community influence, and generational empowerment.

"Legacy is not about what you leave for people; it's about what you leave in people."– Legacy Matters

Through his apostolic anointing, Apostle Howard has helped countless individuals experience the Kingdom's supernatural power—witnessing signs, wonders, and miracles that have broken strongholds and elevated lives. His mission continues to be centered on liberating people, developing leaders, and equipping individuals to maximize their influence for Kingdom advancement.

# Let Me Inspire and Equip Your Team

Bring Amos L. Howard Sr. to Inspire and Equip Your Team

AMOS WILL EMPOWER YOUR TEAM TO ACCOMPLISH IN THE NEXT 12 MONTHS WHAT MANY STRUGGLE TO ACHIEVE IN A LIFETIME.

With over 35 years of transformational pastoral leadership, extensive experience in real estate, and the life-changing principles outlined in his books **Legacy Matters** and **The Earth is Your Real Estate Property**, Amos L. Howard Sr. offers a wealth of wisdom and practical strategies to help individuals and organizations unlock their potential.

LEDGE WITHOUT EXECUTION CREATES NOTHING. GREATNESS COMES FROM ACTION."

While organizations often invest in learning new concepts, the gap between understanding and implementation remains a common barrier to success. Amos bridges that gap by equipping your team with actionable systems rooted in Kingdom principles and practical strategies, ensuring every idea has the power to generate real results.

Whether your team is building legacies in business, faith, or family, Amos delivers:

- **Dynamic Insights:** How to apply legacy-focused strategies that transform lives and organizations.
- **Kingdom Principles for Success:** Learn how to leverage principles from The Earth is Your Real Estate Property to unlock untapped potential.
- **Execution Plans That Work**: Proven methods to translate vision into action and achieve exponential growth.

Session Formats

From a high-impact one-hour keynote to an immersive one-day workshop, Amos's engaging and interactive sessions will inspire your team to think bigger, execute better, and achieve more.

Let Amos L. Howard Sr. show your team how to create lasting impact by turning innovative ideas into measurable outcomes.

Take the first step toward greatness—schedule Amos L. Howard Sr. to speak at your next event. Let's build a legacy together!

At Legacy Builders, LLC, we are passionate about equipping individuals and organizations to create enduring legacies through personal growth, strategic development, and impactful leadership. Our tailored mentorship and training programs are designed to empower you at every stage of your journey.

For many, the greatest barrier to achieving extraordinary success isn't a lack of innovative ideas—it's the resistance to breaking free from entrenched habits and routines. At Legacy Builders, LLC, we recognize that true transformation requires more than just good intentions; it demands ongoing mentorship, strategic guidance, and a commitment to execution.

That's why we offer the 1-Year Legacy Builder Mentorship, a results-driven program designed to help you accelerate growth, maximize impact, and establish a lasting legacy. Research confirms that consistent mentorship dramatically increases the likelihood of success. Our Certified Legacy Builder Mentors are equipped to guide you every step of the way, ensuring that you don't just meet your goals—you surpass them.

A CERTIFIED LEGACY BUILDER MENTOR IS WITH YOU EVERY STEP OF THE WAY, GUIDING YOU TOWARDS YOUR DEFINED LEGACY.

Our mentorship program is designed to support diverse needs, offering:

• **Bi-Weekly Master Classes** – Interactive group sessions providing deep insights, actionable strategies, and peer accountability.

• **Independent Work & Application** – Assignments and exercises to reinforce learning and drive real-world results.

• **2.5-Day Intensive Mastermind Retreats** – Exclusive live experiences designed for breakthrough thinking and implementation.

• **Personalized Mentorship Tracks** – Tailored coaching options for executives, entrepreneurs, and individuals committed to personal and professional transformation.

Whether you're looking to redefine your personal journey, scale your business, or shift your organizational culture, our mentors are here to help you navigate challenges, seize opportunities, and execute at a higher level.

Your legacy won't build itself—let's create it together.

At Legacy Builders, LLC, we are committed to providing comprehensive support to individuals and organizations aiming to build lasting legacies. Explore our range of tailored products and services designed to elevate your potential:

• **1-Year Legacy Builder Mentorship:** Dive deep into a year-long journey where personal growth meets strategic guidance. This mentorship program is designed to help you create a lasting impact, offering personalized insights and actionable strategies.

• **Consulting Services:** Tap into our expertise with customized consulting solutions that address the unique challenges and opportunities within your organization. Our consultants are dedicated to helping you achieve exceptional results.

• **Train the Trainer:** Empower your team with our Train the Trainer program. This initiative equips leaders like you with the skills and knowledge to effectively train others, enhancing overall organizational performance.

• **Online Video Courses:** Access our library of online video courses at your convenience. These courses cover a wide range of topics, all curated to foster skills development and personal growth at your own pace.

For more information and to take the next step towards greatness, simply scan the QR code below and discover how our proprietary tools and programs can be leveraged to your greatest advantage.

# Also by Amos L. Howard, Sr.

**<u>The Earth is Your Real Estate Property</u>**

**Contact Information:**

Church Name: Living Truth Christian Center

Address: 102 Ridley Street Smyrna, TN 37167

Email: info@apostlehoward.com

Church numbers: Office: 615-459- 9017, Other: 615-624-1327

**Follow Amos Howard, Sr. on Social Media:**

Youtube: AmosHowardSr

Instagram: AmosHowardSr

Facebook: Living Truth Christian Center & BreakThrough Ministry

Made in United States
North Haven, CT
10 November 2026

22088893R00124